LEEDS ART GALLERY

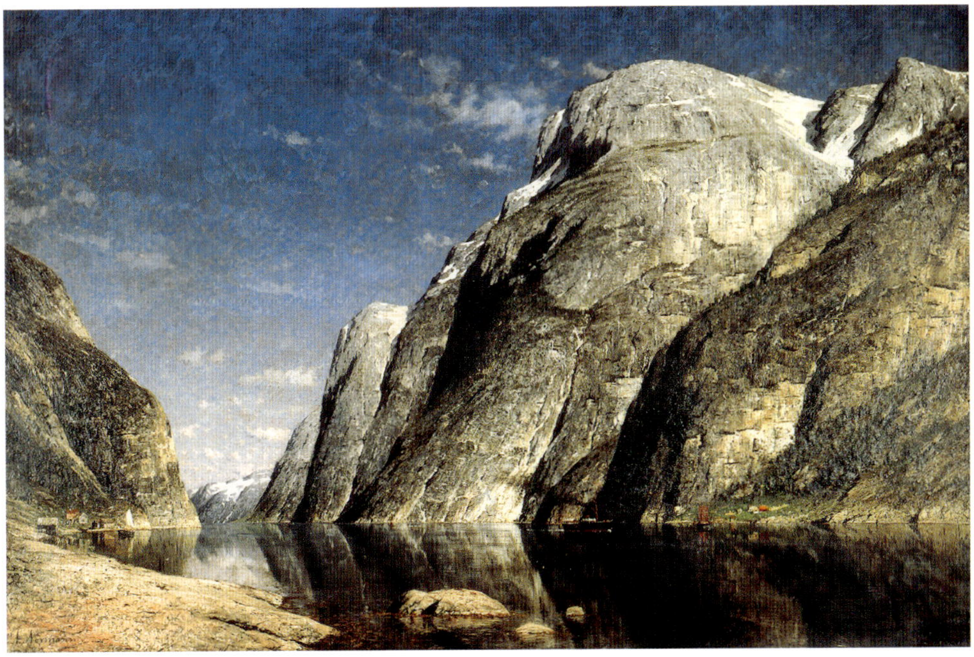

LEEDS MUSEUMS & GALLERIES

Front cover: Antony Gormley's *Maquette for the Leeds Brick Man* (photograph by Monty Rakusen)

Title page: Adelsteen Normann, *The Sognefjord* (1885)

Back cover: Henry Moore's *Reclining Woman '80 No.1* at the entrance to the Gallery

ISBN 0 901981 75 3

Published 2007 by Leeds Museums & Galleries,
c/o Discovery Centre, Carlisle Road, Leeds LS10 1LB
Telephone 0113 214 1548

Text by Alexander Robertson, Corinne Miller and Sophie Raikes
Designed by FDA, Huddersfield
Printed by J W Northend Ltd, Sheffield

Introduction to Leeds Art Gallery, its History and Collections

Following the opening of the new Town Hall in 1858, a strategy emerged in Leeds to create an art gallery. It was said that Colonel TW Harding stood for election to the Council in order to facilitate this. After the opening of the Municipal Buildings in 1884 incorporating the new Central Library, the decision was taken to add an art gallery, designed by WH Thorp, onto the building, to be entered through a magnificent sculpture court. Funds from the Queen's Golden Jubilee launched the appeal and within a year the building was ready. It opened on 3 October 1888.

Initially, the collection was very small, incorporating gifts made to the town since 1858: the JG Uppleby bequest including Panini and Gainsborough Dupont and works donated by Harding and his friends, contributed from their own collections. H M the Queen lent Lady Butler's famous painting *The Roll Call* to the opening exhibition. New incandescent lighting was mentioned as a feature of the Gallery.

The first Curator, George Birkett, was an indefatigable organiser, endeavouring to build up a collection with only very limited financial resources, but lots of goodwill from the art world. The decision to buy contemporary art was probably a sensible one, as it was readily available and often at modest cost.

By 1898 the first catalogue of paintings and drawings had been produced, as well as a catalogue of the sculpture casts. By the time of the sixth edition in 1906 there were 228 works in the five Gallery rooms.

The difficulties of buying anything, with decisions having to be agreed by Committee, led to the establishment of a friends organisation in 1912, called the Leeds Art Collections Fund, which took its name from the national counterpart founded in 1903. The annual subscription was one guinea.

The First World War led to a partial evacuation of the Gallery collections and the housing of Belgian refugees in dormitories upstairs. In spite of the war, two notable events for the Gallery took place. Firstly, the establishment of the Alfred Bilbrough bequest in 1915, which enabled the Gallery to acquire English watercolours and, in 1918, the bequest

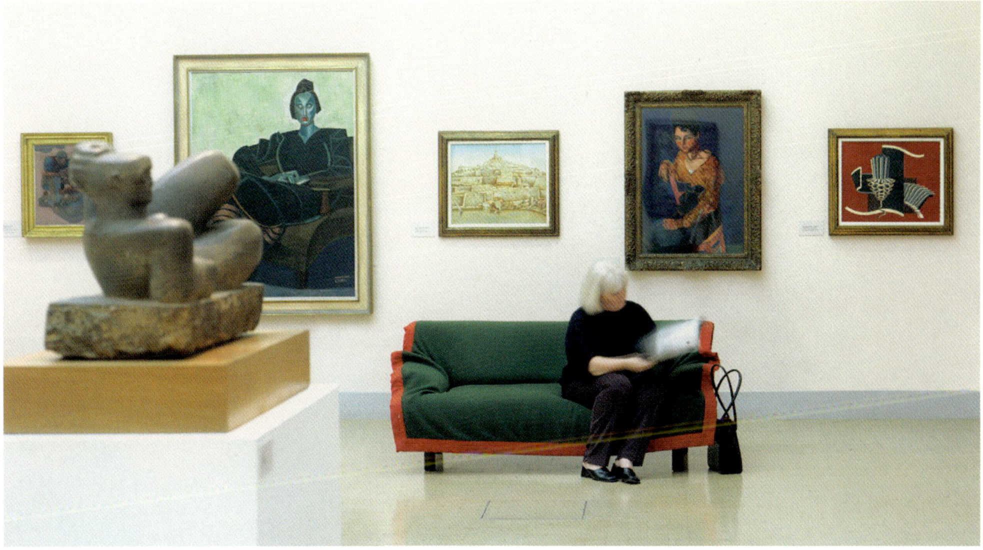

Fig. 1 The West Room with a selection of early 20th century works from the collection

from Sam Wilson, a notable Leeds woollen manufacturer, of his entire collection of early 20TH century British paintings, sculpture, ceramics and furniture. He had already presented a set of Frank Brangwyn's murals bought from the British Pavilion at the Venice Biennale of 1906 to the Gallery and now over three hundred works of art, including canvases by William Orpen, Mark Senior, George Clausen and John Buxton Knight came to the Gallery in a purpose-built series of rooms housed in an extension to the Art Gallery, opened in 1925.

By 1920 the Gallery collection was established as mainly a British Victorian and Edwardian art collection, with a growing number of English watercolours. In that year the Jewish Community of Leeds presented Jacob Kramer's *The Day of Atonement* of 1919, the most modern British painting to enter the Gallery up to that time. However, during the Directorship of Philip Hendy, 1934–1945, collecting took a significant turn away from what had become traditional and conservative, towards art which reflected decidedly new developments. Hendy actively supported the 'moderns' such as Henry Moore, Barbara Hepworth, Ben Nicholson, Stanley Spencer, Graham Sutherland, as well as Walter Sickert and Edward Wadsworth.

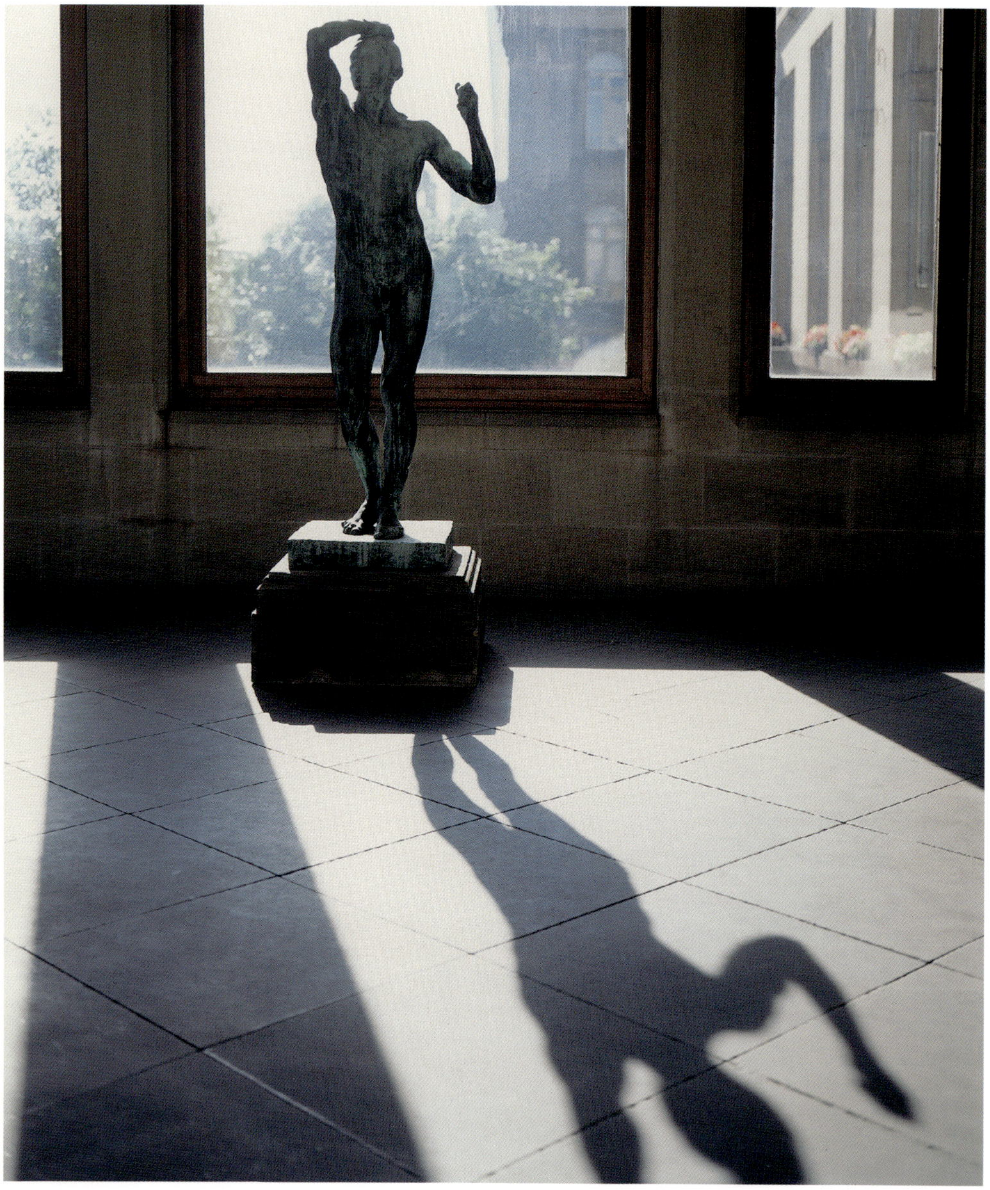

Fig.2 The Age of Bronze (1877)
Auguste Rodin (1840–1917)
cast 1907, bronze, height 178cm
in the entrance

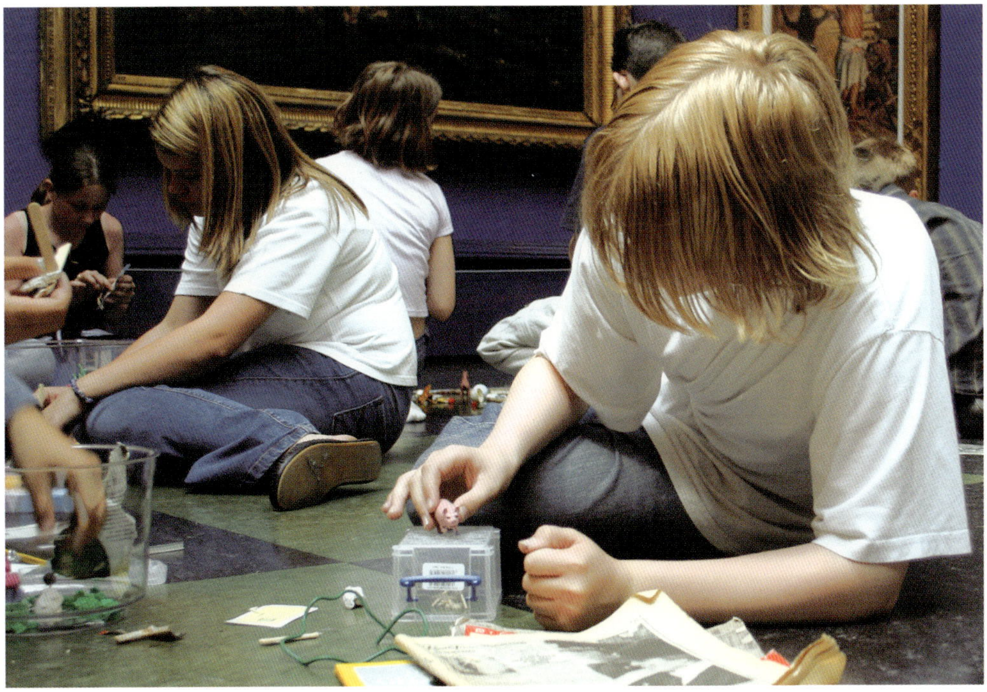

Fig.3 Educational activity in the Ziff Gallery

During the second evacuation of the Gallery collections in the 1939–1945 war, he organised a series of pioneering exhibitions at Temple Newsam House, which established Leeds as a centre for contemporary British art. In 1938 the Sydney Kitson bequest of drawings and watercolours, mostly by John Sell Cotman, was made to the Gallery, further enhancing the works on paper collection and in 1949 and 1952 the Agnes and Norman Lupton collection of over five hundred English watercolours and prints entered the collection, leading to the provision of a special Print Room and Art Library which opened in 1961.

In the 1950s and 1960s new trends in contemporary art were represented with the establishment of the Gregory Fellowships (an artist in residence scheme) at Leeds University, which brought young painters, sculptors, poets and musicians to the city. New works were acquired by artists, including pieces by Terry Frost, Hubert Dalwood, Alan Davie and John Walker amongst others. In 1958 a dedicated Sculpture Gallery was constructed within the building which facilitated the development of this aspect of the collection. Most notably, a new 'front door' was opened onto Victoria Gardens in 1952, giving independent access to the building for the first time.

The need for more space and the condemning of the upper floors of the building led to plans for a new extension and refurbishment. The resulting Moore Gallery opened in 1982 and the rear extension of 1986 enhanced the Gallery's facilities to include a new Print Room, Education Room and café. By the year 2000, the British sculpture collection was second only to the Tate Gallery, London in breadth and importance. As the new millennium arrived, the Contemporary Art Society's Special Collections Scheme offered the chance to develop other aspects of modern art, enabling the purchase of installation pieces and video art. In 2007, the Gallery underwent further refurbishments. The original Victorian Tiled Hall connecting it to the Central Library was restored and reopened with a new café and shop. A new temporary exhibition space was created in the old Art Library and the former café area was transformed into the Art Space.

Victorian Art

Victorian art of an academic nature was the main focus for the collection from 1888 until 1920.

The death of Leeds stockbroker Thomas Plint in 1861 deprived the Gallery of possible masterpieces from his collection, particularly of the Pre-Raphaelite School, which might have come its way if Plint had lived longer. So Holman Hunt's *Shadow of Death* filled an important gap when it arrived in 1903 from the executors of Charles George Oates.

George Birkett, the first Curator, spent much of his time writing to artists asking for biographical information or negotiating prices. There does not seem to have been a written acquisitions policy for purchases, but by 1920 the Victorian era was well represented by a cross-section of paintings featuring the various categories of subject matter and techniques which were a feature of the annual Royal Academy Summer Exhibition. George Bernard O'Neill's *Public Opinion* shows a crowd at a popular exhibition, pushing forward to see the year's star attraction. Other contemporary events such as the war in Afghanistan and the fighting in the Sudan were represented by *The Drums of the Fore and Aft* and *The Death of General Gordon*.

As there was no regular purchase grant for acquiring new work, money had to come from the remains of the Jubilee Fund and then from the Technical Education Grant from London. In many cases great paintings by the leading artists of the day were far too expensive for the Council's means, so it was left to Colonel Harding and his friends to contribute what they could in the way of significant works of art as gifts or bequests. The valiant Colonel also gave sums of money for future purchases in 1925 and 1927.

The Royal Academy Summer Exhibition provided a source for new art, albeit of an academic kind, and the Leeds Spring Exhibition often contained unsold work from the previous year's London show, doing the rounds of the provinces hoping for a buyer. From such a show came the extraordinary *The Sognefjord* by Adelsteen Normann, delivering large spectacular-scale drama to the spectator. Other paintings presented romantic medieval stories (Arthur Hacker's *Temptation of Sir Percival)* or classical myths (Lord Leighton's *The Return of Persephone)* on the walls of the Gallery or, more rarely, the tragedy of every-day life (Holl's *The Village Funeral*) all with the aim of 'educating and improving' the visitor. In the early years, with few other attractions in Leeds, the Art Gallery provided a popular place of entertainment and even glamour, achieving visitor figures of 420,303 in the year 1896–1897.

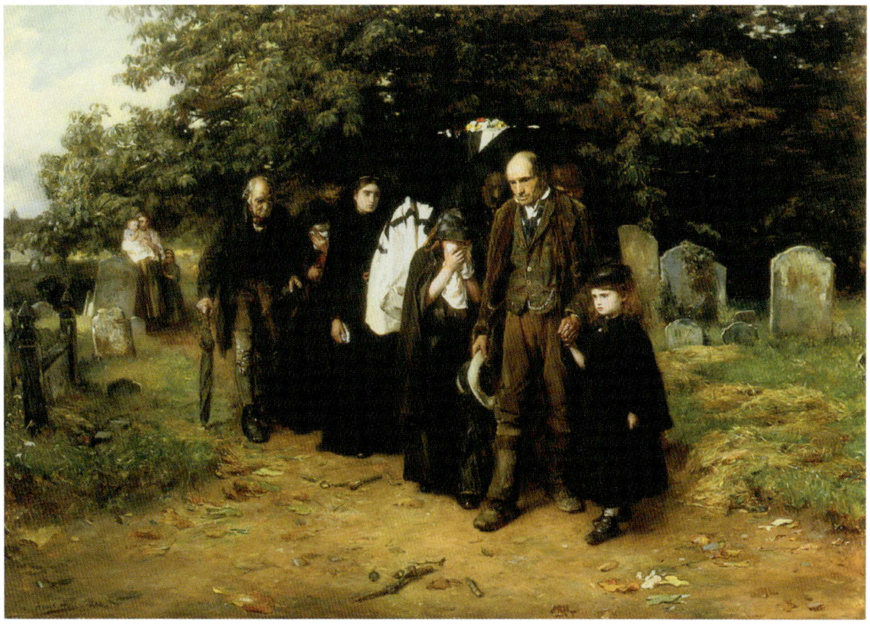

I am the Resurrection and the Life (The Village Funeral) 1872

Frank Holl (1845–1888)

Oil on canvas 116.8 x 162.6cm
Bought 1894

Famous for his early social realist subjects, Holl later turned to portraiture. This is one of the few scenes of contemporary life in the collection. Engraved in *The Graphic* magazine, Vincent Van Gogh owned a copy of the print

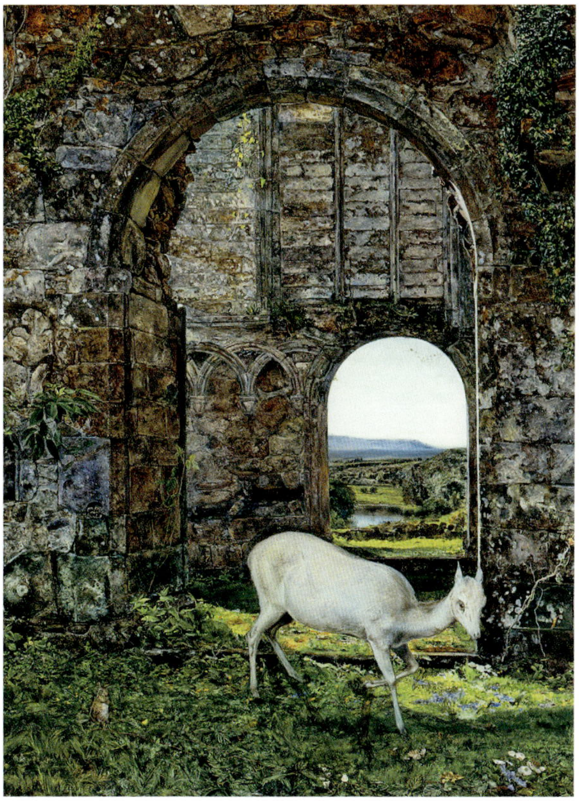

At Bolton (The White Doe of Rylstone) 1855

John William Inchbold (1830–1888)

Oil on wood 68.6 x 50.8cm
Given by Ernest Inchbold 1934

A true Pre-Raphaelite landscape, showing amazing clarity and details thus observing Ruskin's dictum of 'truth to nature'

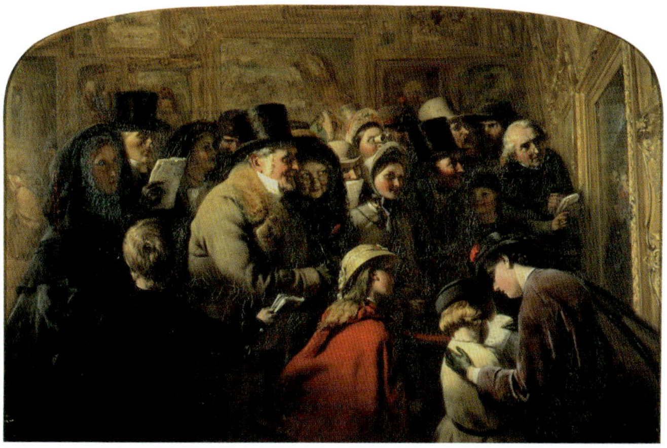

Public Opinion c1863

George Bernard O'Neill (1828–1917)

Oil on canvas 53.2 x 78.8cm
Given by the friends of the late J W Middleton 1888

A cross-section of Victorian society admiring the 'painting of the year' at the Royal Academy Summer Exhibition

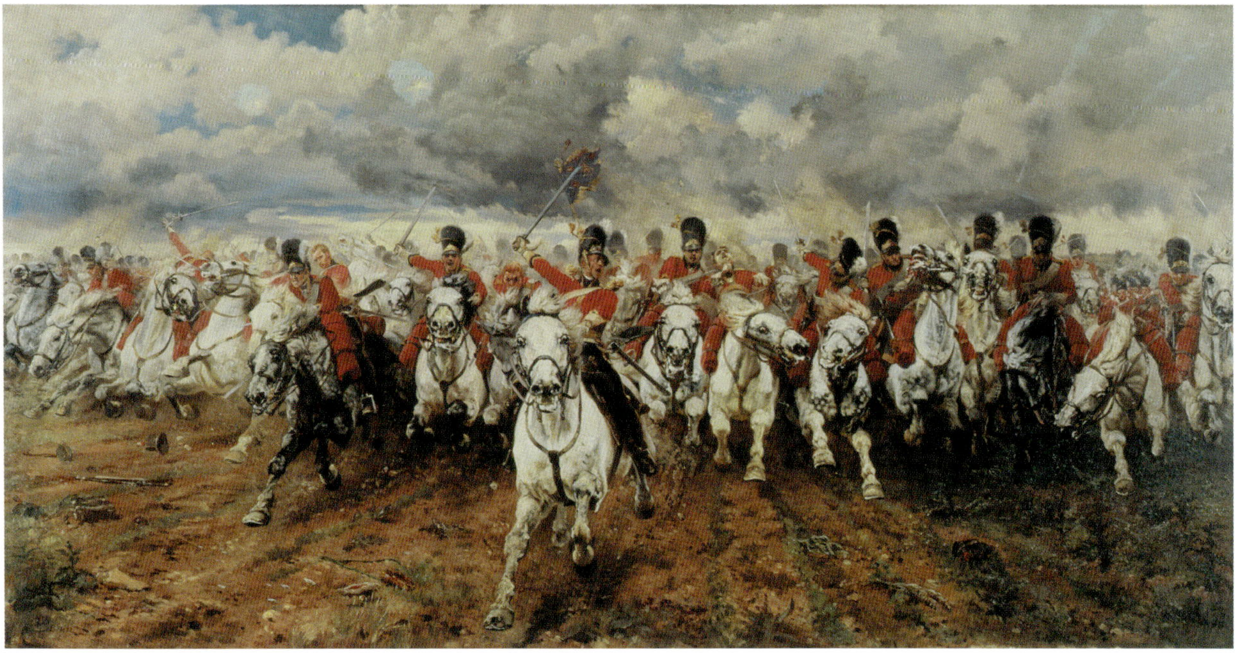

Scotland for Ever! 1881

Lady Elizabeth Butler (1846–1933) Oil on canvas 101.6 x 194.3cm Given by Colonel TW Harding 1888

One of the Gallery's most famous paintings, *The Charge of the Scots Greys at the Battle of Waterloo* (1815) was bought by Colonel TW Harding and presented to the Gallery in 1888

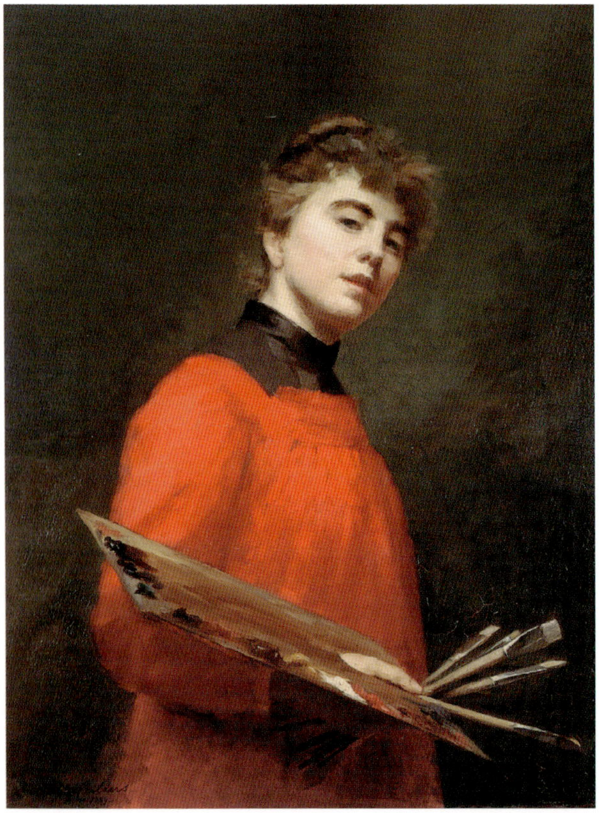

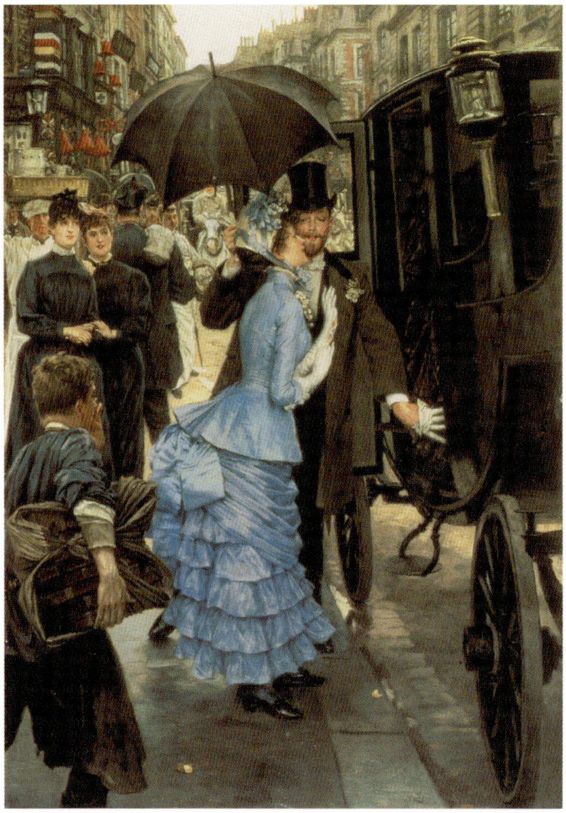

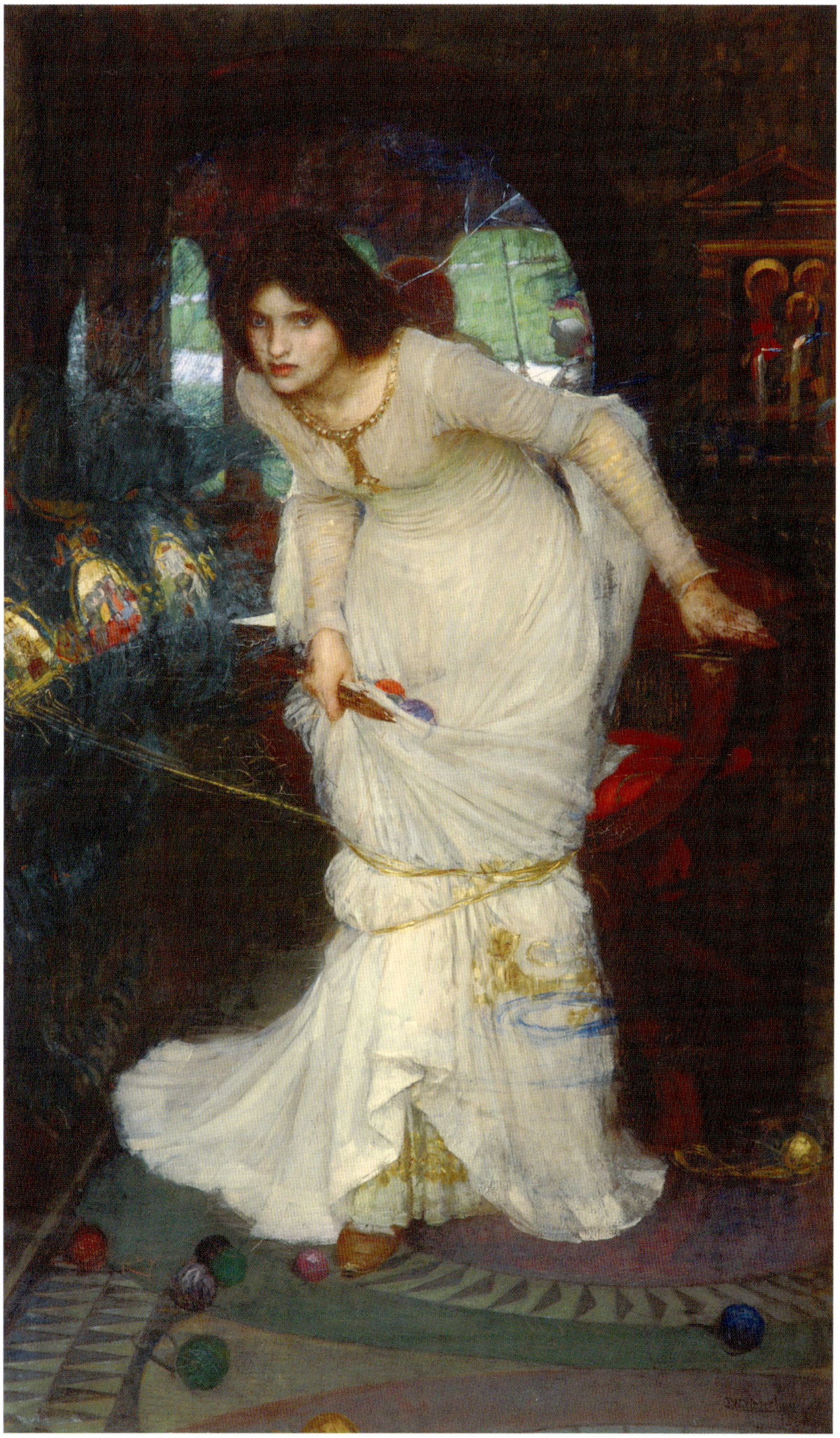

OPPOSITE BOTTOM LEFT

Self Portrait 1889

Emily (Milly) Childers (active 1888–1922)

Oil on canvas 92 x 68cm
Given by Miss E Deane 1937

Daughter of politician Hugh Culling Eardley Childers, Milly worked for Lord Halifax at Temple Newsam House, Leeds before the First World War

OPPOSITE BOTTOM RIGHT

The Bridesmaid c1885

James Tissot (1836–1902)

Oil on canvas 147.3 x 101.6cm
Given by RR King 1897

From the series *La Femme à Paris.* Tissot revelled in painting glamorous society events and modern life subjects

The Lady of Shalott 1894

John William Waterhouse (1849–1917)

Oil on canvas 142.2 x 86.3cm
Bought 1895

Based on a verse from Tennyson's *Idylls of the King*:

Out flew the web and floated wide
The mirror cracked from side to side
'The curse is come upon me' cried
The Lady of Shalott

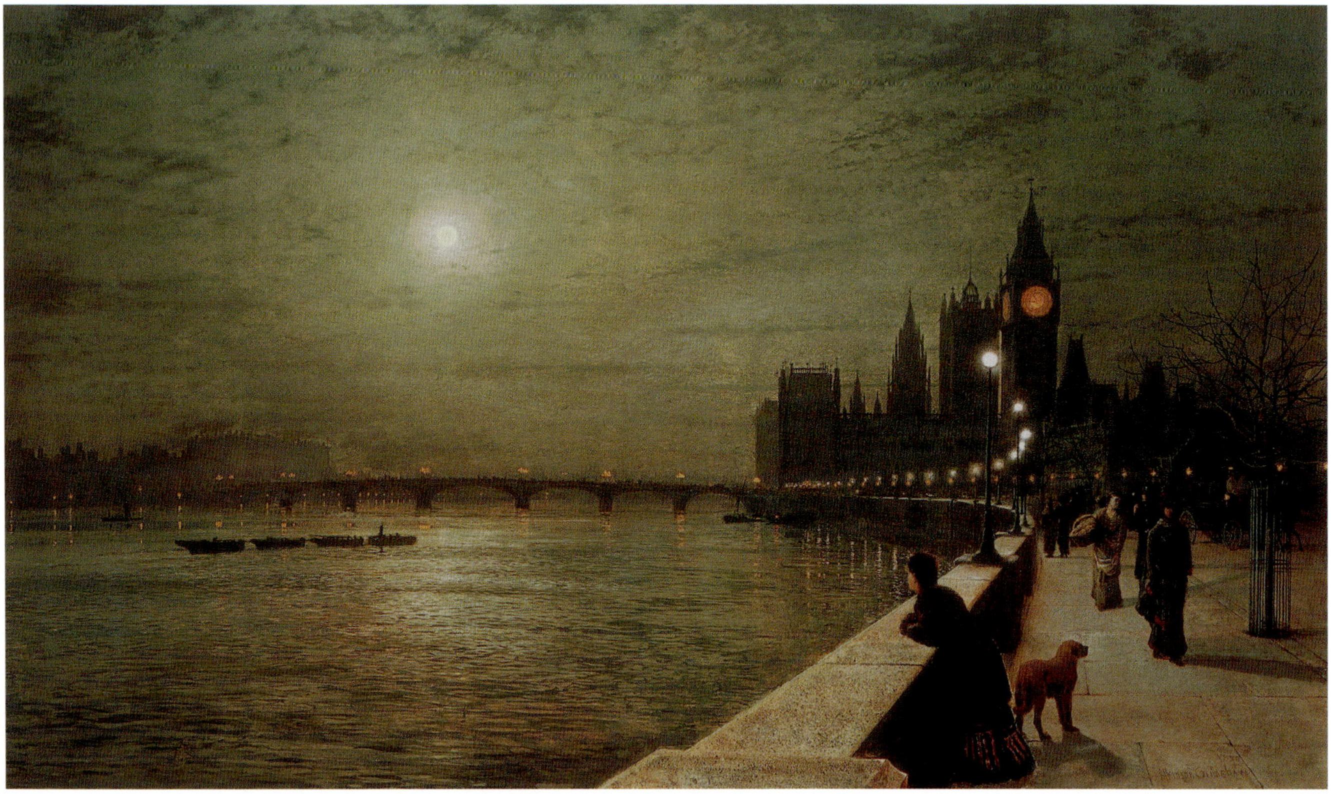

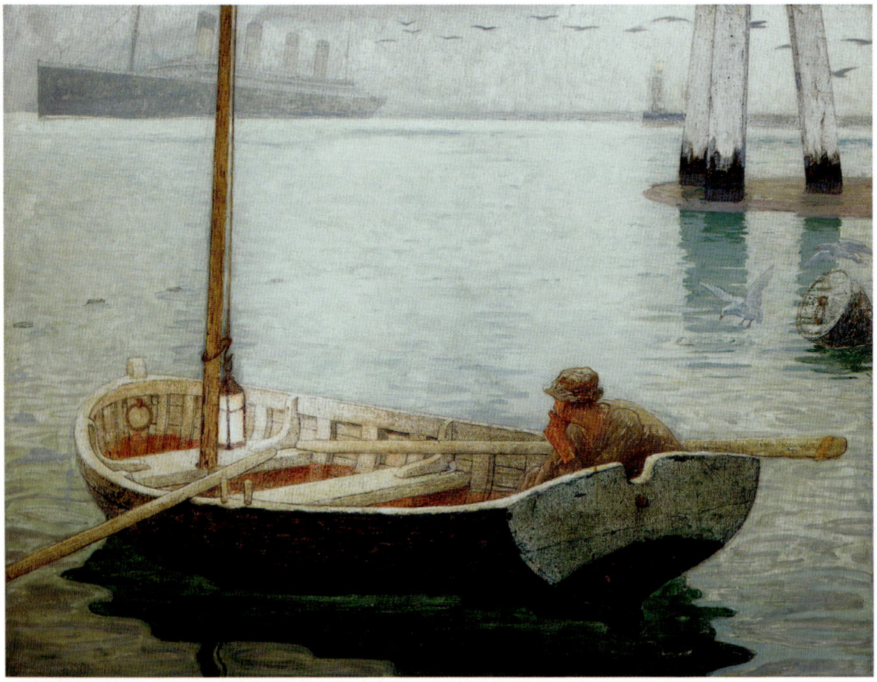

ABOVE

Reflections on the Thames, Westminster 1880

John Atkinson Grimshaw (1836–1893)

Oil on canvas 76.2 x 127cm
Given by J Kirk 1900

This embankment scene shows the new electric lighting

The Outward Bound 1912

Frederick Cayley Robinson (1862–1927)

Oil on canvas 71.1 x 91.4cm
Given by Professional Musicians of Leeds

Commissioned by the Musicians of Leeds to commemorate the loss of their colleagues on the SS Titanic, April 1912

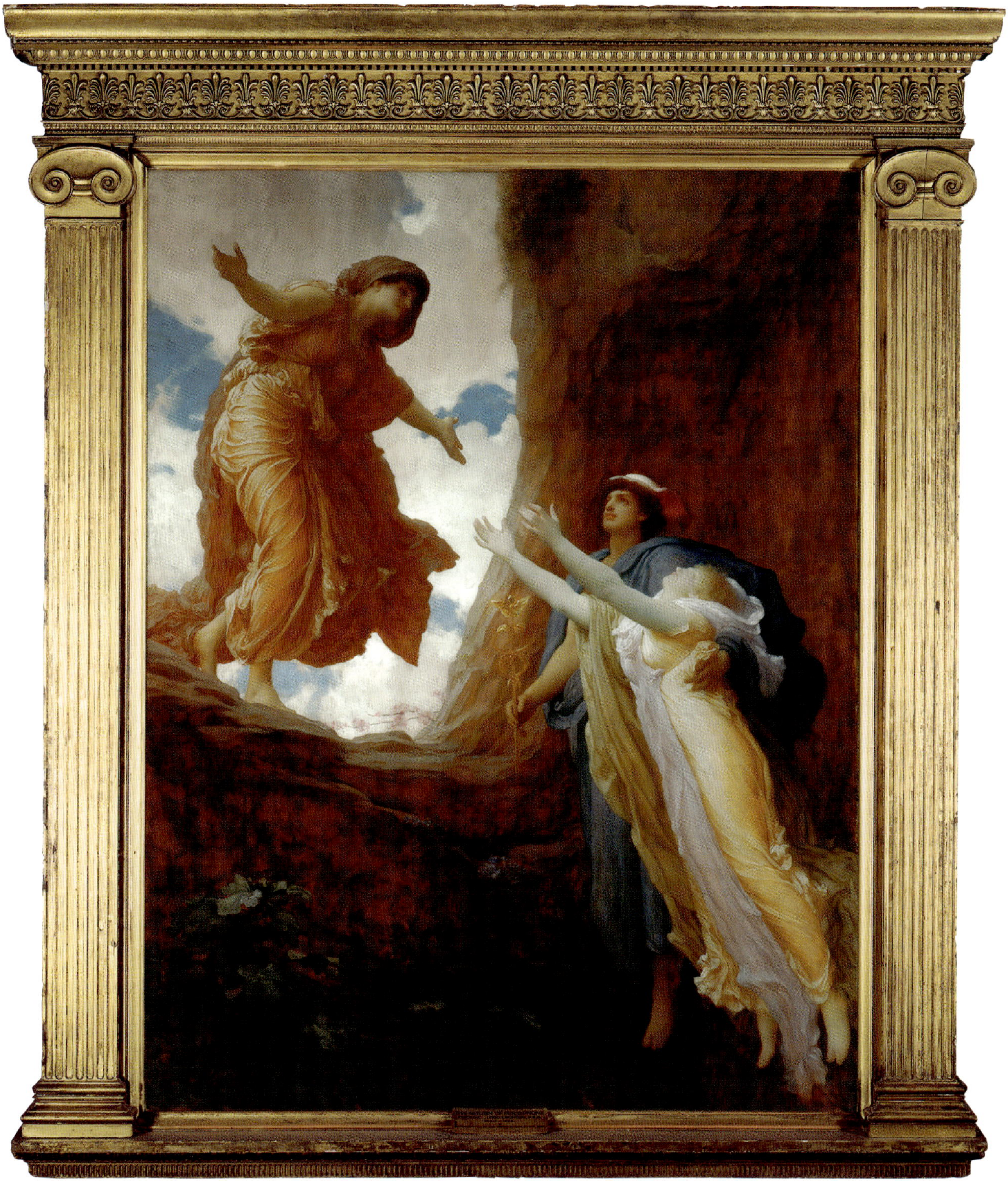

The Return of Persephone c1891

Frederic Lord Leighton (1830–1896)

Oil on canvas 203 x 152cm Given by Sir James Kitson 1891

This great painting (an allegory of Spring) is a masterpiece of the High Victorian Renaissance

British and French Painting 1800–1900

The 19TH century saw one of the most decisive changes in art practice since the Renaissance. A complete revolution in art technique took place, from late-Romanticism through Realism to Impressionism. The dramatic change can be seen by comparing John Crome's *Wherries on the Yare* to André Derain's *Barges on the Thames*. Established principles covering perspective, modelling, light and shade and natural colour were radically altered and a new language created.

The driving factors were both a desire for 'natural' landscape or 'real' landscape, leading to *plein-air* or outdoor painting, and a desire to capture 'truth to nature' where every leaf, twig, moss-covered stone was painstakingly shown. This itself led to a new method of painting which sought to catch the moment, using a new painting method which became known as 'Impressionism'.

The success of John Constable at the Paris Salon of 1824 was part of this evolving change away from the classical Claudian picture, with its carefully controlled low tones and artificially organised composition. Landscape needed re-vivifying. In the 19TH century this often took the form of new subject matter, either looking at subjects in far-away places or by setting up artist colonies in locations such as the Forest of Fontainebleau near Paris. (A major collection of French art of the Barbizon school was given to the Gallery by Charles Roberts in 1937).

By the 1870s changes in painting methods went hand in hand with new subject matter: modern life, the everyday world of Paris, its streets, river and night-life. Picture sizes also tended to be more domestic in scale and geared less to the grand Academy Exhibition. No more scenes of romantic heroines or classical gods; Mr and Mrs Anybody were just as interesting as medieval legends. After the first Impressionist exhibition in Paris in 1874 there was an increasing move towards a new aesthetic, a new painting language which would produce more radical changes in the early years of the 20TH century. In England the Royal Academy still remained the official centre of artistic effort, but even there the signs of change were evident as artists began to absorb new ideas. More avant-garde societies like the New English Art Club were established, while artists James McNeil Whistler and Walter Sickert advocated a more 'art for art's sake' approach to painting.

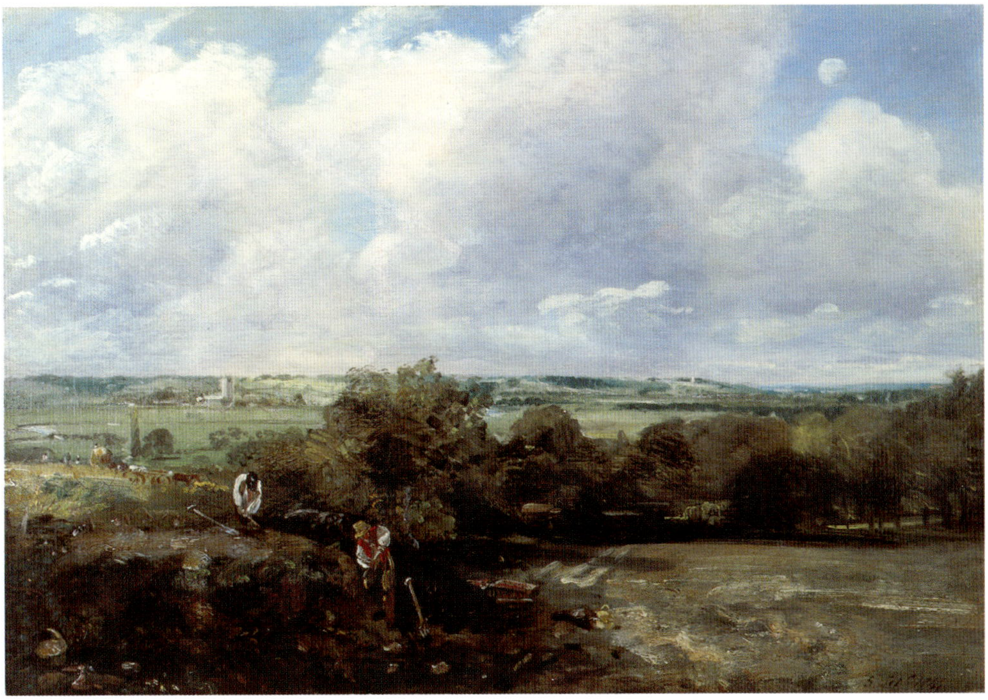

The Vale of Dedham 1814
John Constable (1776–1837)
Oil on canvas 39.4 x 55.9cm
Bought 1934

Constable's fresh and breezy landscape is an oil study for the much larger painting in Boston, Mass. Here the very naturalism of the scene shows a final break with classicism

On the River Yare 1807
John Sell Cotman (1782–1842)
Oil on canvas 42.5 x 33.6cm
Given by the Leeds Art Collections Fund 1934

From the 'Greta' period, Cotman's love of shape and pattern is here imposed on the natural forms of the riverscape

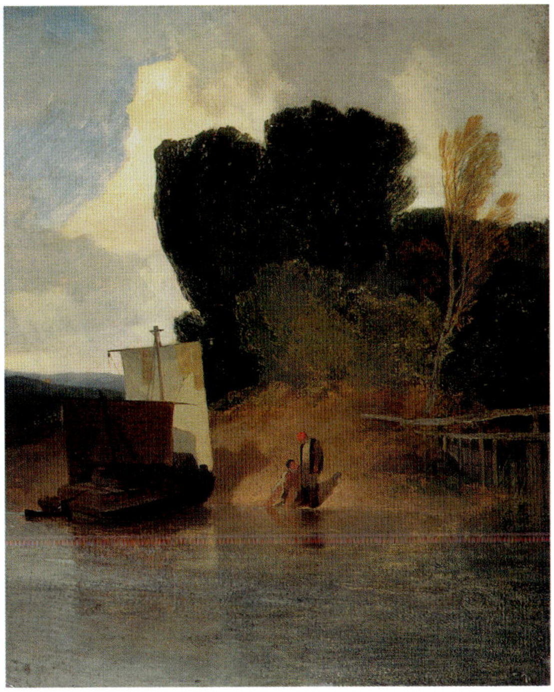

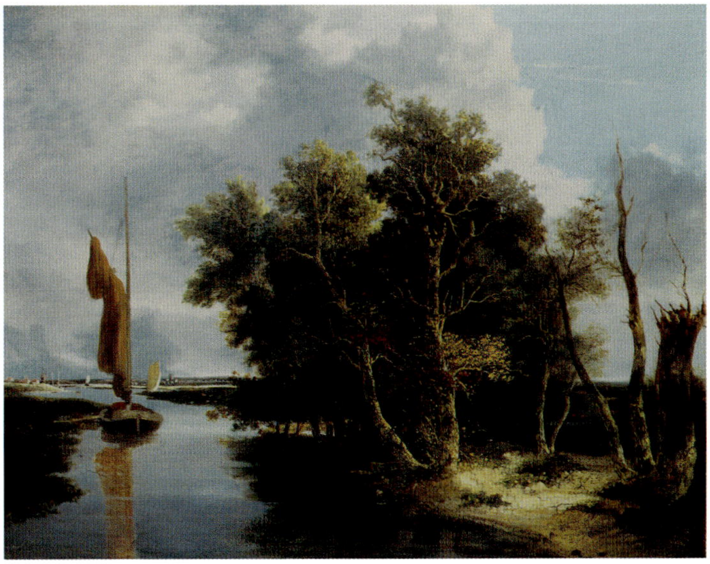

Wherries on the Yare c1810
John Crome (1768–1821)
Oil on canvas 48.2 x 59.7cm
Given by S Smith 1935

Leader of the Norwich School, Crome adapted a Dutch 17TH century landscape to views of the similar flatlands of Norfolk

Storm near Montmartre

Georges Michel (1763–1859)

Oil on canvas 68.6 x 138.5cm
Given by Sir Michael Sadler through The Art Fund 1931

Another artist who was deeply influenced by Dutch landscape painting; here Rembrandt is certainly the model

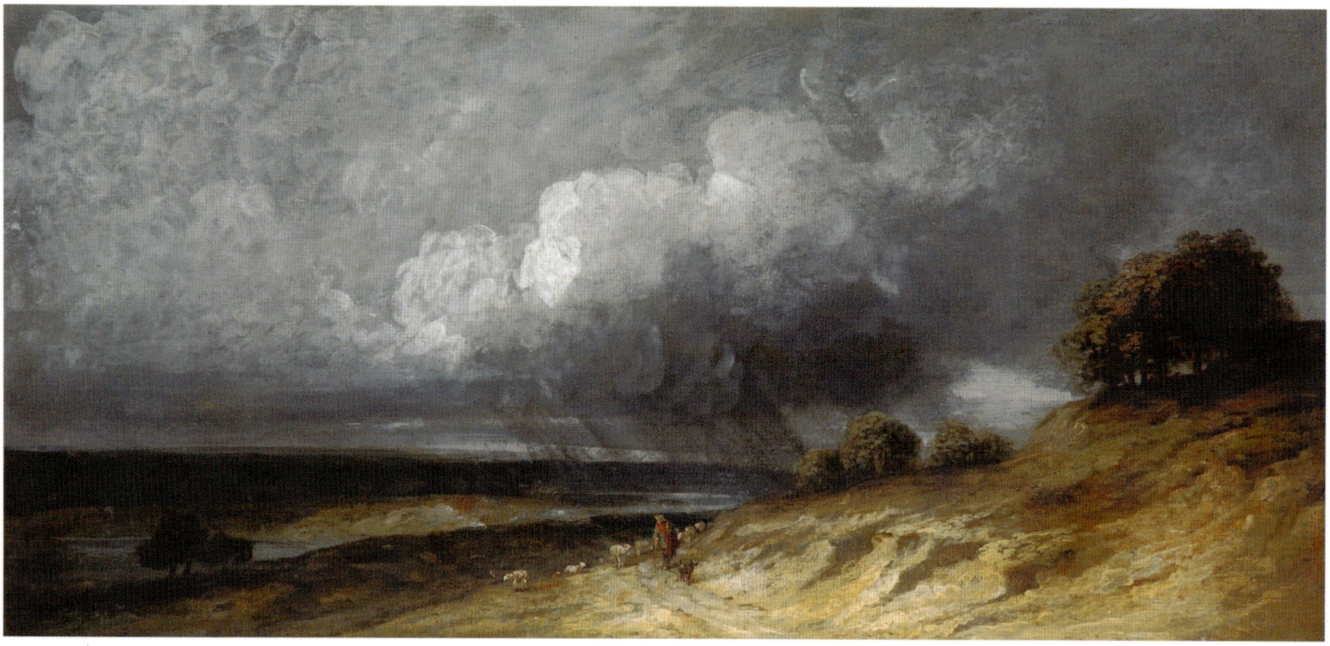

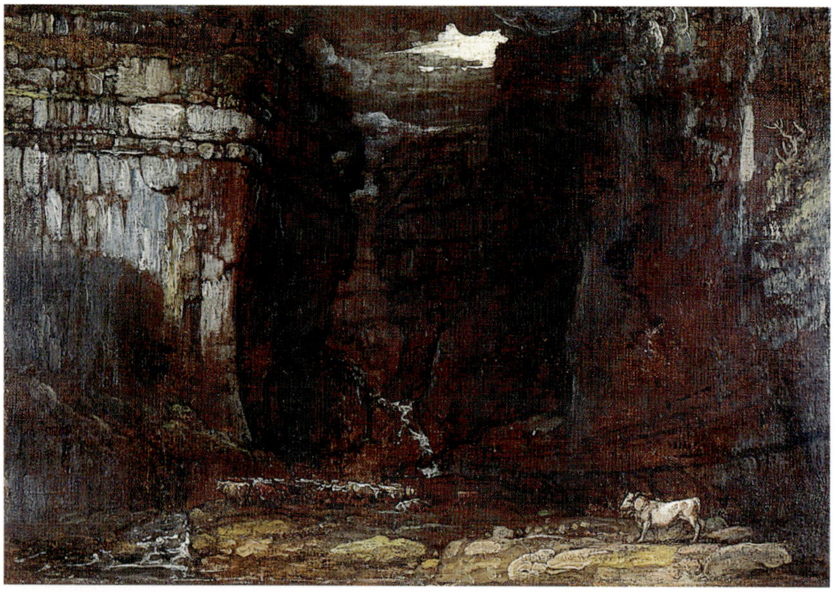

Study for 'Gordale Scar' c1811–13

James Ward (1769–1859)

Oil on canvas 38.1 x 55.9cm
Bought 1942

Ward produced two finished versions of this subject, seen as a comment about nature and the elements

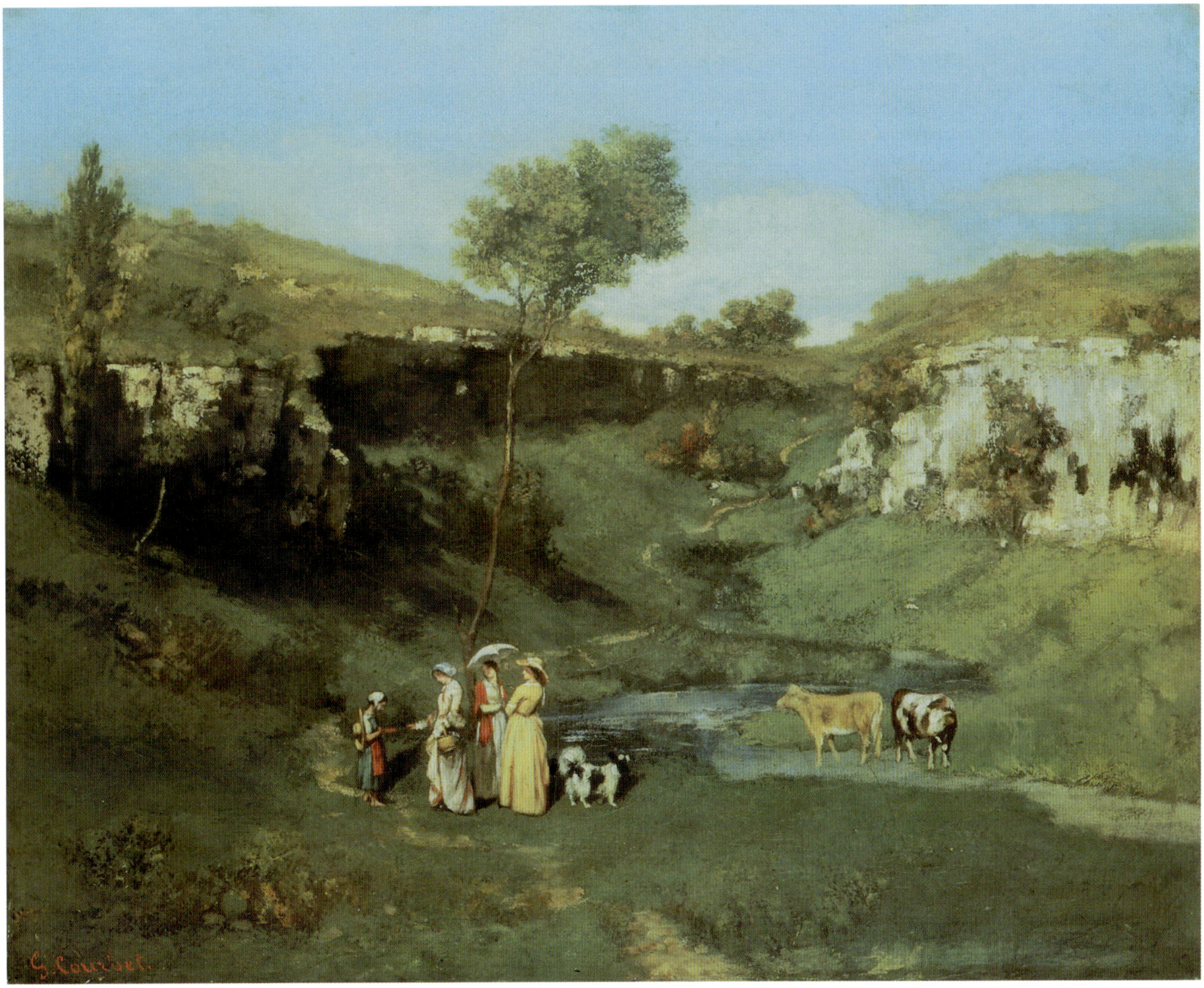

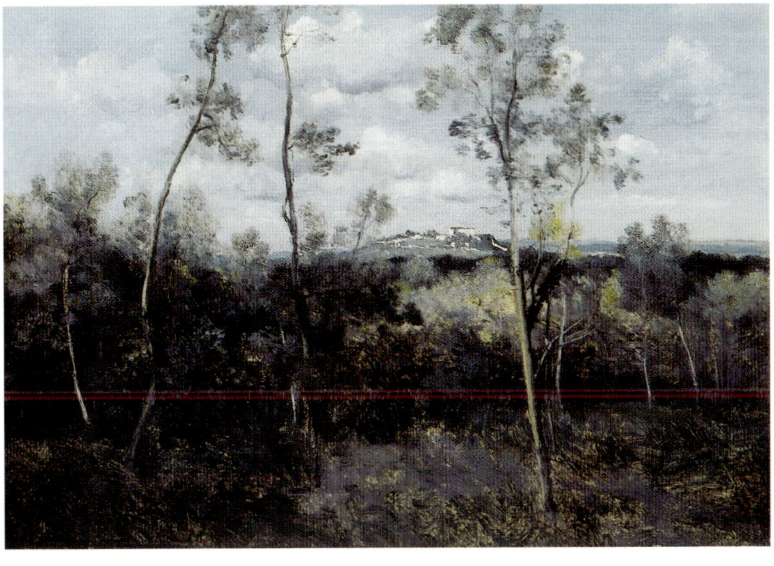

ABOVE

The Young Ladies of the Village 1851

Gustave Courbet (1819–1877)

Oil on canvas 54 x 65.4cm
Charles Roberts bequest 1937

Courbet's resolute stand against the establishment and his depiction of the poor on a heroic scale led to a lifetime's notoriety. His landscapes often contain paint laid on with a palette knife. His searing colours show a break with traditional low tonality

The Mont Valerian c1835

Camille Corot (1796–1875)

Oil on wood 24.5 x 34.2cm
Agnes and Norman Lupton bequest 1952

A superb example of Corot's ability to show a magical sylvan glade on a summer's day

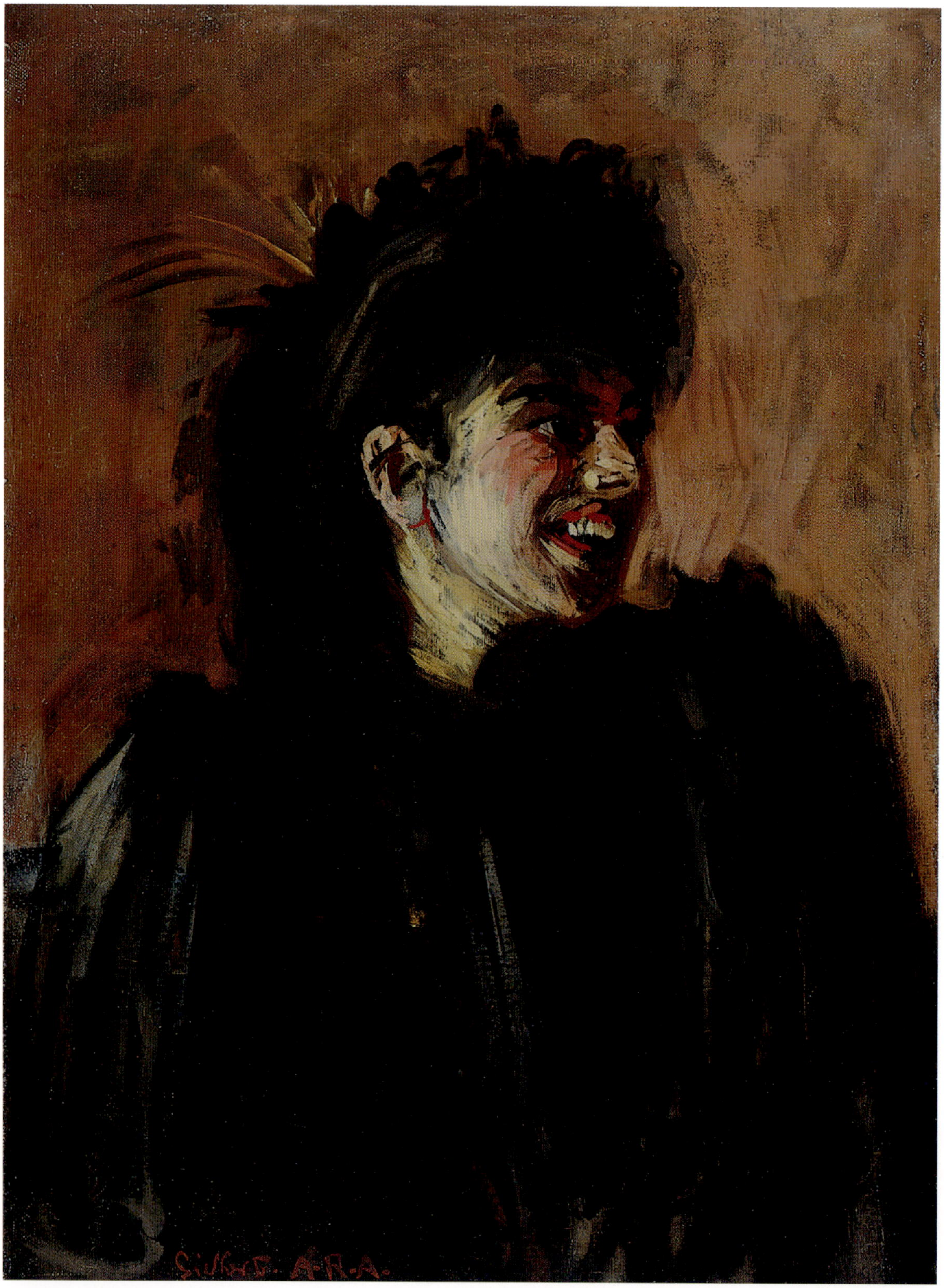

The Blackbird of Paradise c1896–98

Walter Richard Sickert (1860–1942)

Oil on canvas 66 x 48cm

Bought 1945

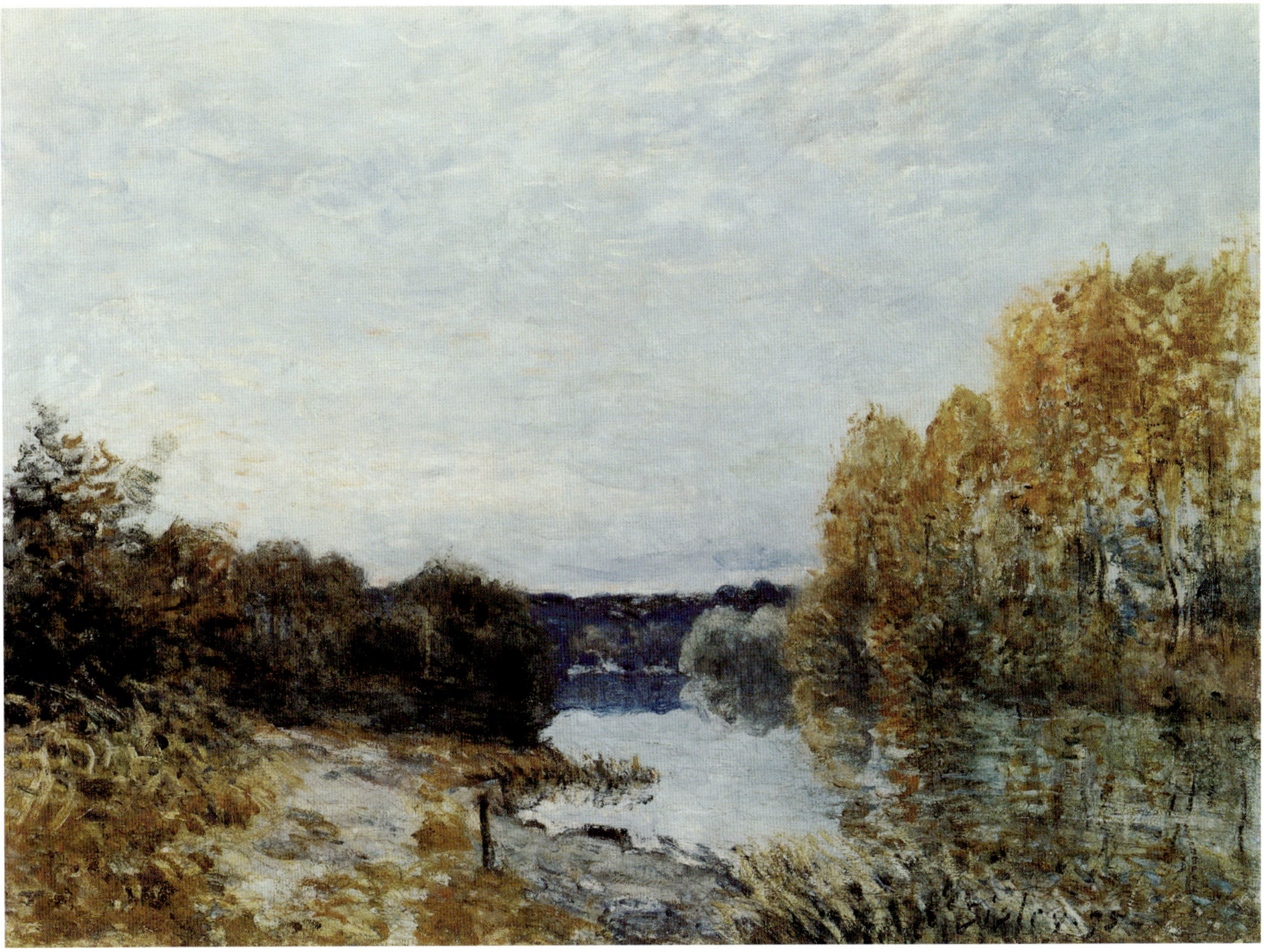

ABOVE

Autumn Evening on the River 1875

Alfred Sisley (1839–1899)

Oil on canvas 46 x 61cm
Given by Mrs DM Fulford through
The Art Fund 1945

Painted in the year after the first Impressionist exhibition was held

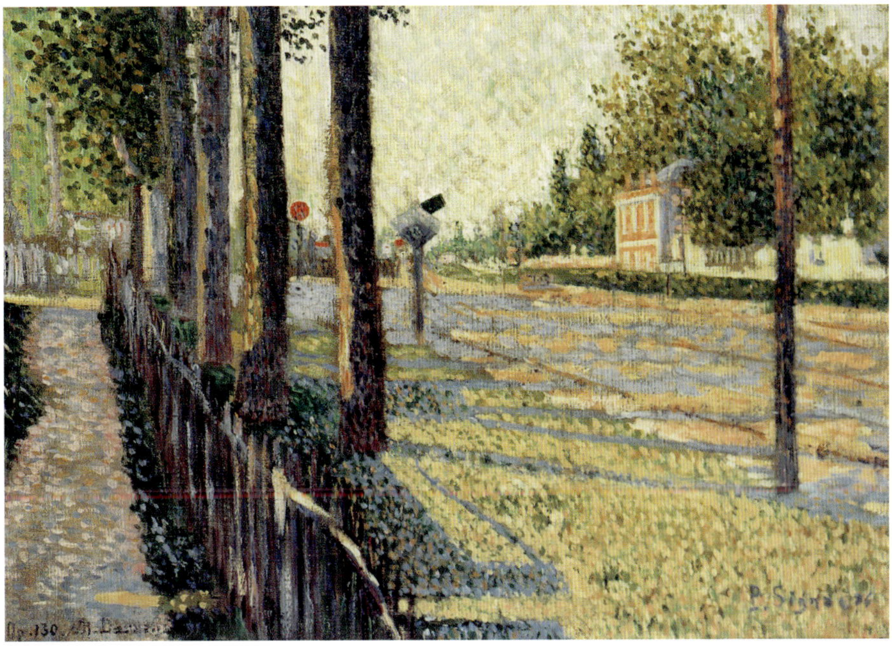

The Railway Junction at Bois-Colombes (La Route Pontoise) 1886

Paul Signac (1863–1935)

Oil on canvas 33 x 47cm
Bought 1948

Shown in 1886 at the last Impressionist exhibition. The underlying structure of the painting is reinforced by a surface made up of organised dabs of colour

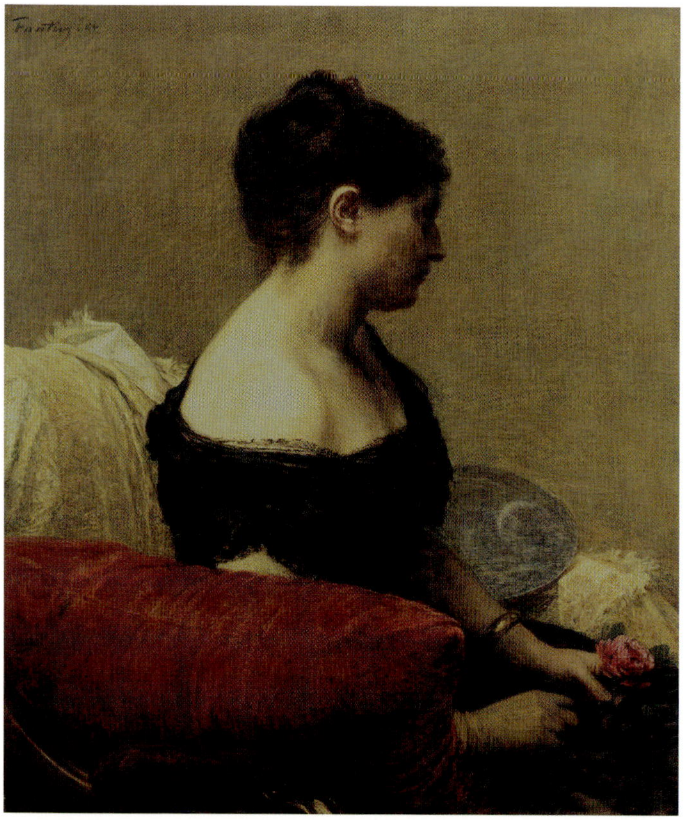

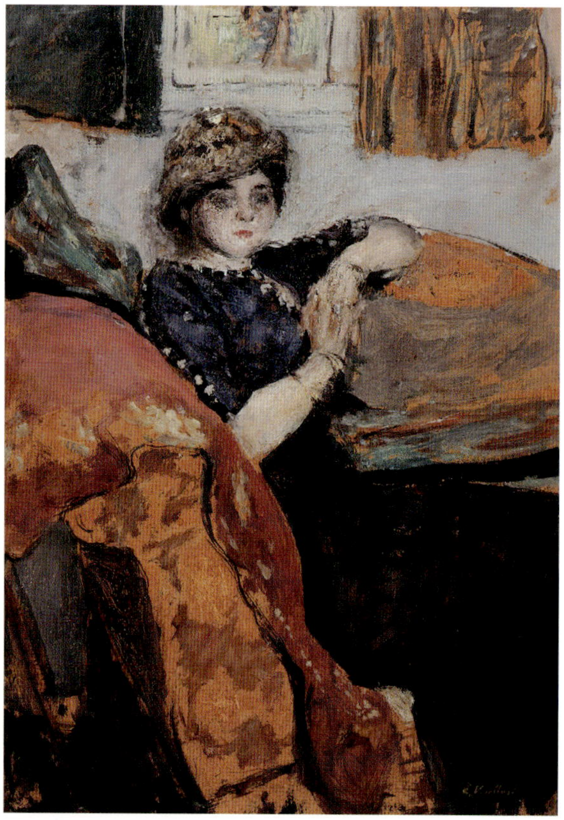

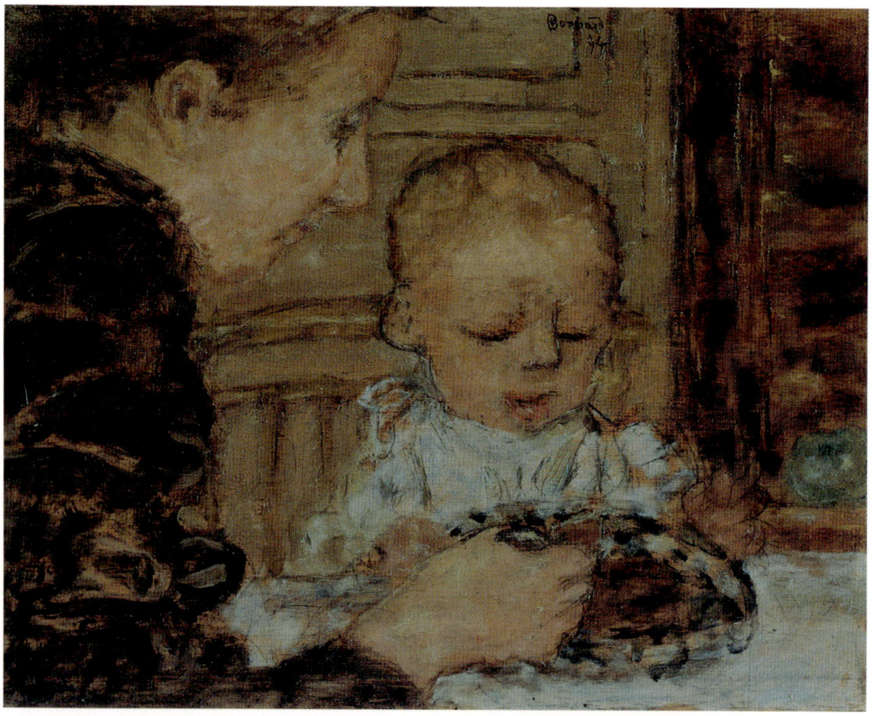

ABOVE LEFT

Portrait of Mme Leon Maitre 1884

Henri Fantin-Latour (1836–1904)

Oil on canvas 85.7 x 74.3cm
Charles Roberts bequest 1937

A daring portrait of the wife of a friend where the light effects and colours are the main subject

ABOVE RIGHT

Mlle Grandidier in the Artist's Studio c1912

Edouard Vuillard (1868–1940)

Oil on board 56 x 34.3cm
Bought 1945

Grandmother and Child 1894

Pierre Bonnard (1867–1947)

Oil on wood 34.4 x 41.9cm
Bought by the Leeds Art Collections Fund 1939

An intimate family study

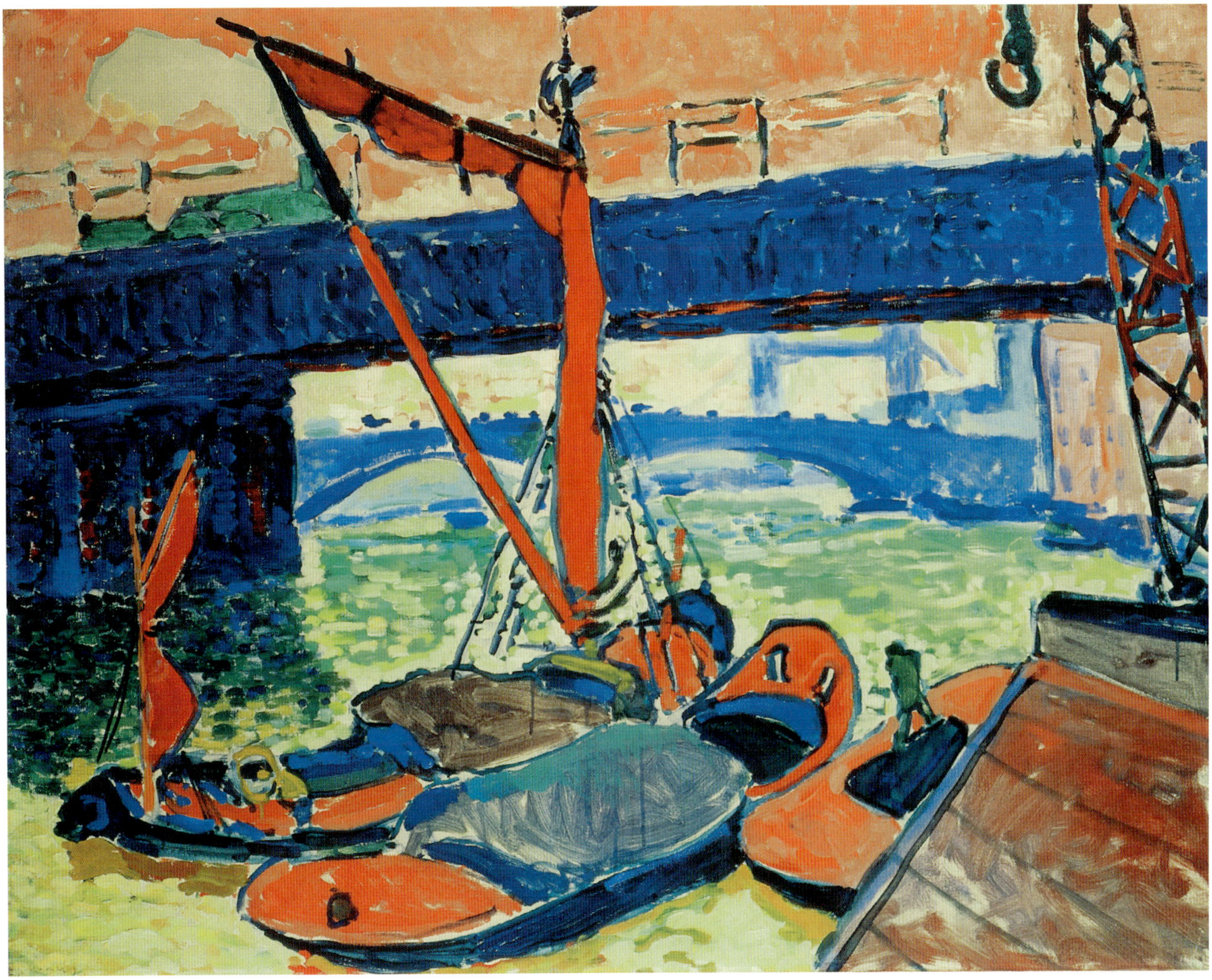

Barges on the Thames 1906

André Derain (1880–1954)

Oil on canvas 81.3 x 99cm
Bought 1937

As one of 'Les Fauves', (the Wild Beasts), Derain here abandons all conventional ideas of traditional perspective, modelling with light and shade and natural colour. It is a defiant statement for the early 20TH century. Bought by the Gallery in the year the Director Philip Hendy secured an annual purchase grant from the local council, the painting still has the power to surprise

British Art 1900–1920

One of the most vibrant periods in European and British art, these two decades saw the final ousting of the Royal Academy as the arbiter of taste and the emergence of British artists fully aware of thirty years of artistic change in other parts of Europe.

The return of Walter Sickert to London in 1905 and the grouping around him of young artists who admired Monet, Cézanne and Van Gogh, whose subjects and painting methods defied those with a more conservative attitude, came to be known as the Camden Town Group. The immense Allied Artists Exhibitions staged at the Albert Hall from 1908 revealed the rich diversity of talents (in the first year alone there were 3061 exhibits). At this time in London, at the Slade School, several young artists arrived who were keen to produce new 'modern' art, challenging academic practice: Mark Gertler, David Bomberg, Stanley Spencer and Leeds artist Jacob Kramer were part of this fresh approach.

In many ways, what happened in London was a reaction, a catching up with continental practices, but often a paler imitation of it. The new 'isms' in art followed one after another: Post-Impressionism, Fauvism, Cubism, Futurism, Dadaism and, in England, a native variation of Cubism and Futurism which came to be known as Vorticism – the vortex of art. New ideas in art, music, politics and literature led to a frenzied, amazingly rich period of history until suddenly brought crashing down by the First World War. In Leeds the Gallery's innovative Curator, Frank Rutter, went to work at the Admiralty in London. Artists were called up. The horror of the trenches outdid anything art could imagine. Paul Nash captured some of the sense of desolation and destruction in his war paintings and prints, but the thirst for novelty and innovation was stopped in its tracks except for the activities of the Dadaists in Zurich.

Even so, several trends remained to be followed up later. The move towards abstraction and pure form; while the revolutionary anarchic experiments of Dada remain inspirations to artists even now. By 1920 the Art Gallery received its last Victorian painting for many years, Herbert Draper's reduced replica of *Ulysses and the Sirens*.

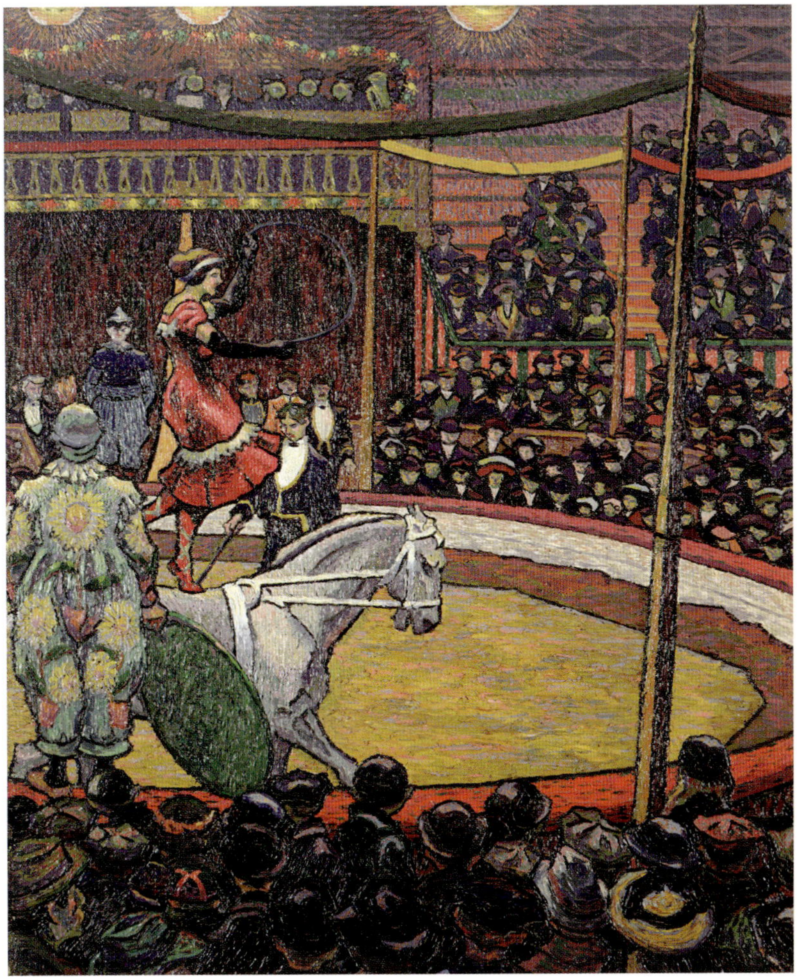

The Circus c1913

Charles Ginner (1878–1952)

Oil on canvas 60.7 x 50.7cm
Bought 1976

Set in the Agricultural Hall, Islington, London, *The Circus* shows the influence of French Post-Impressionist painting on Ginner's technique, with its thick impasto and images reminiscent of Van Gogh

BELOW LEFT

The Balcony, Mornington Crescent c1911

Spencer Gore (1878–1914)

Oil on canvas 60.9 x 50.8cm
Bought 1949

Along with Charles Ginner and Harold Gilman, Gore was a founder member of the Camden Town Group, a circle of young artists gathered around Walter Sickert

BELOW RIGHT

Portrait of Mrs Mounter c1916–17

Harold Gilman (1878–1919)

Oil on canvas 33 x 17.9cm
Bought 1934

Mrs Mounter was Gilman's landlady in Maple Street, London

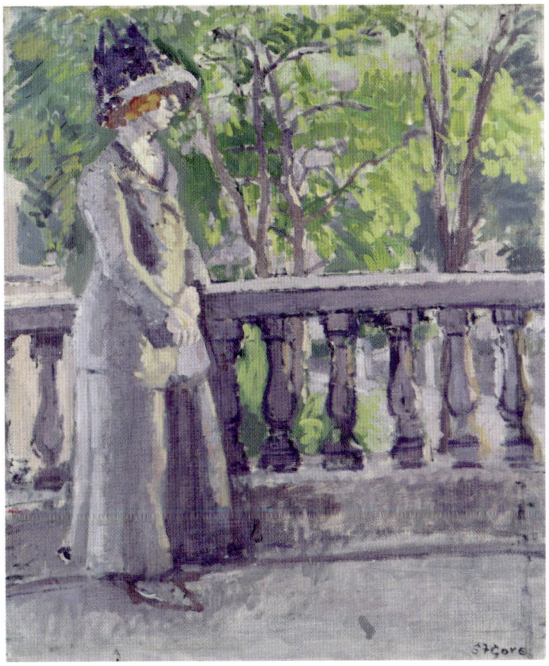

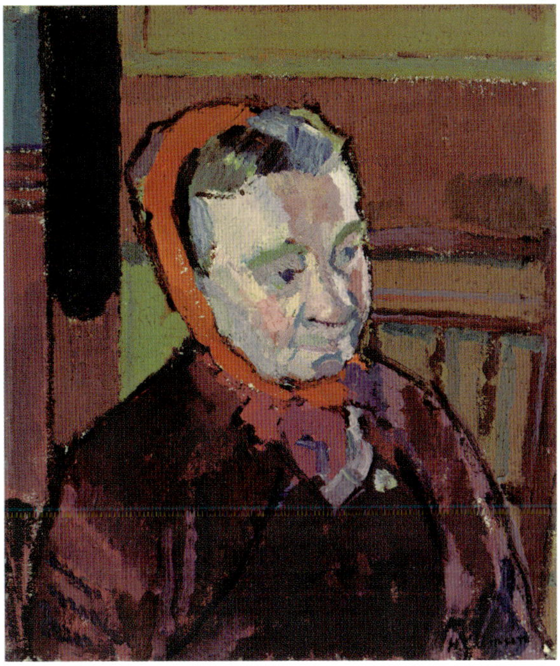

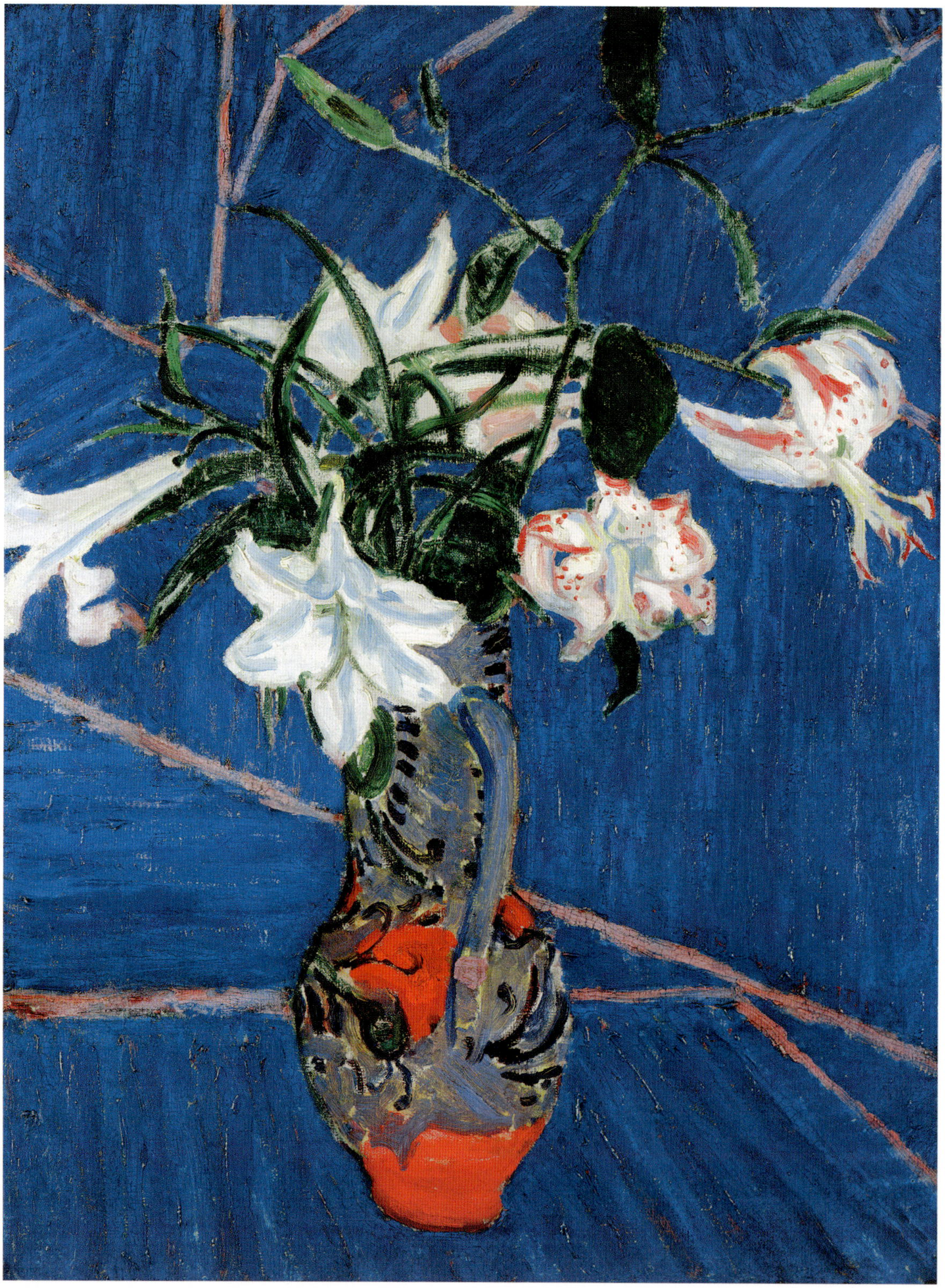

Lilies c1913–14

Sir Matthew Smith (1879–1959)

Oil on canvas 73.6 x 53.2cm Bought 1939

Smith's earliest painting to be exhibited in England, at the London Group in 1916. The vibrant, singing colours show the artist's debt to Islamic pottery and the colour of French artist Henri Matisse

The Pond, Garsington 1916
Mark Gertler (1891–1939)
Oil on canvas 63.3 x 63.3cm
Bought 1941

The faceted paint surface shows the growing influence of a cubistic style

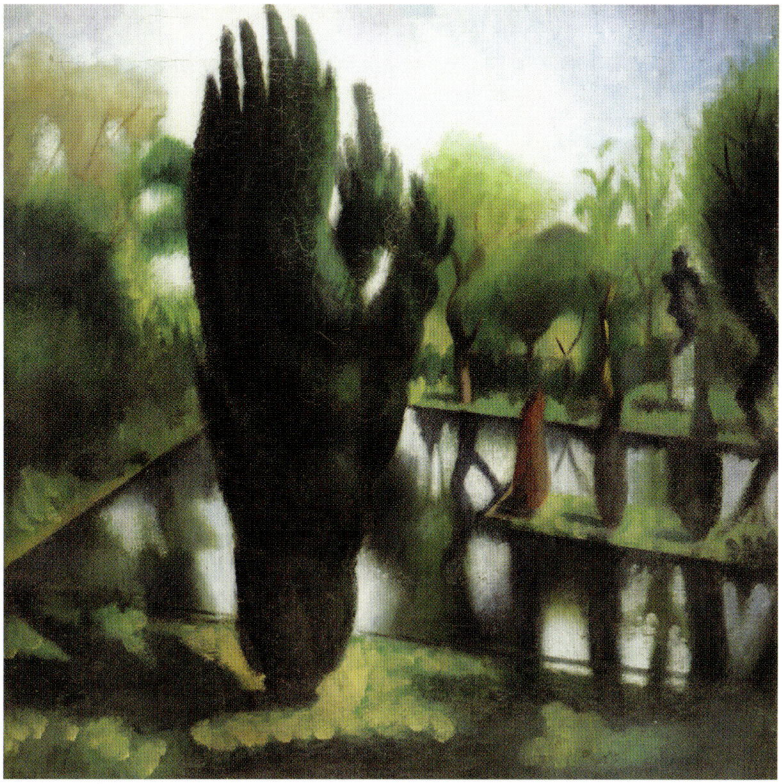

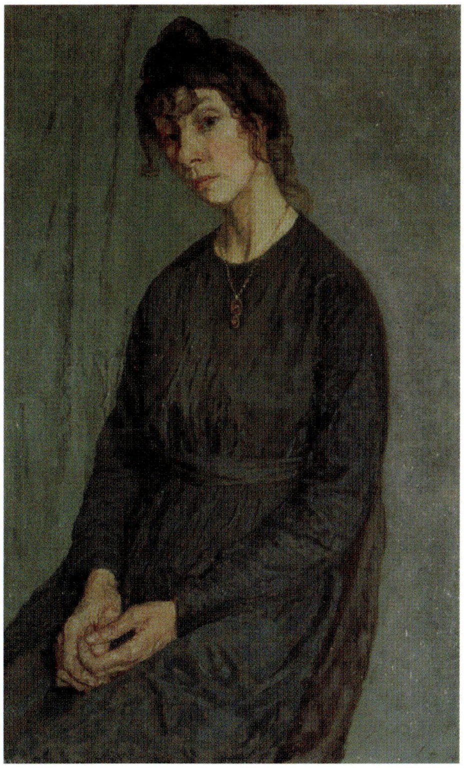

Portrait of Chloe Boughton-Leigh c1910–14
Gwen John (1876–1939)
Oil on canvas 60.3 x 38.6cm
Bought 1955

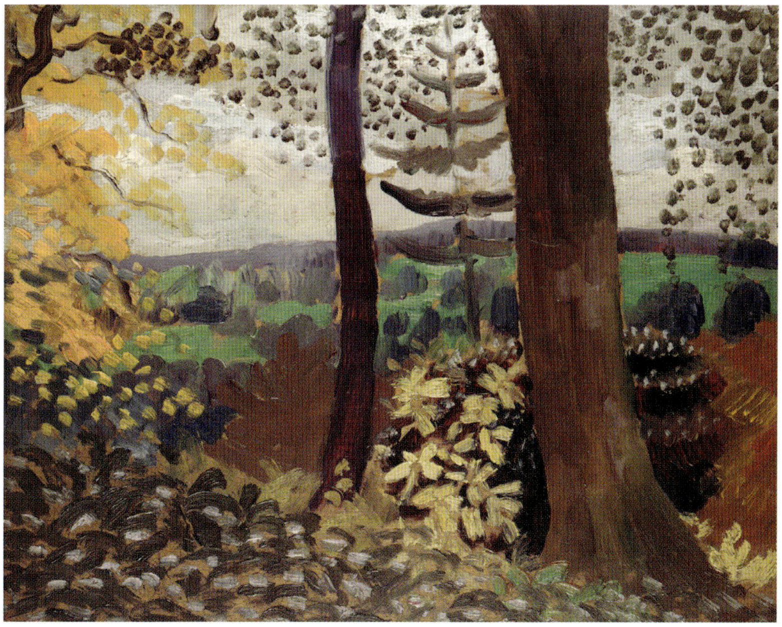

Landscape at Chirk 1911–12
Augustus John (1878–1961)
Oil on wood 33 x 40.6cm
Given by HM Hepworth 1934

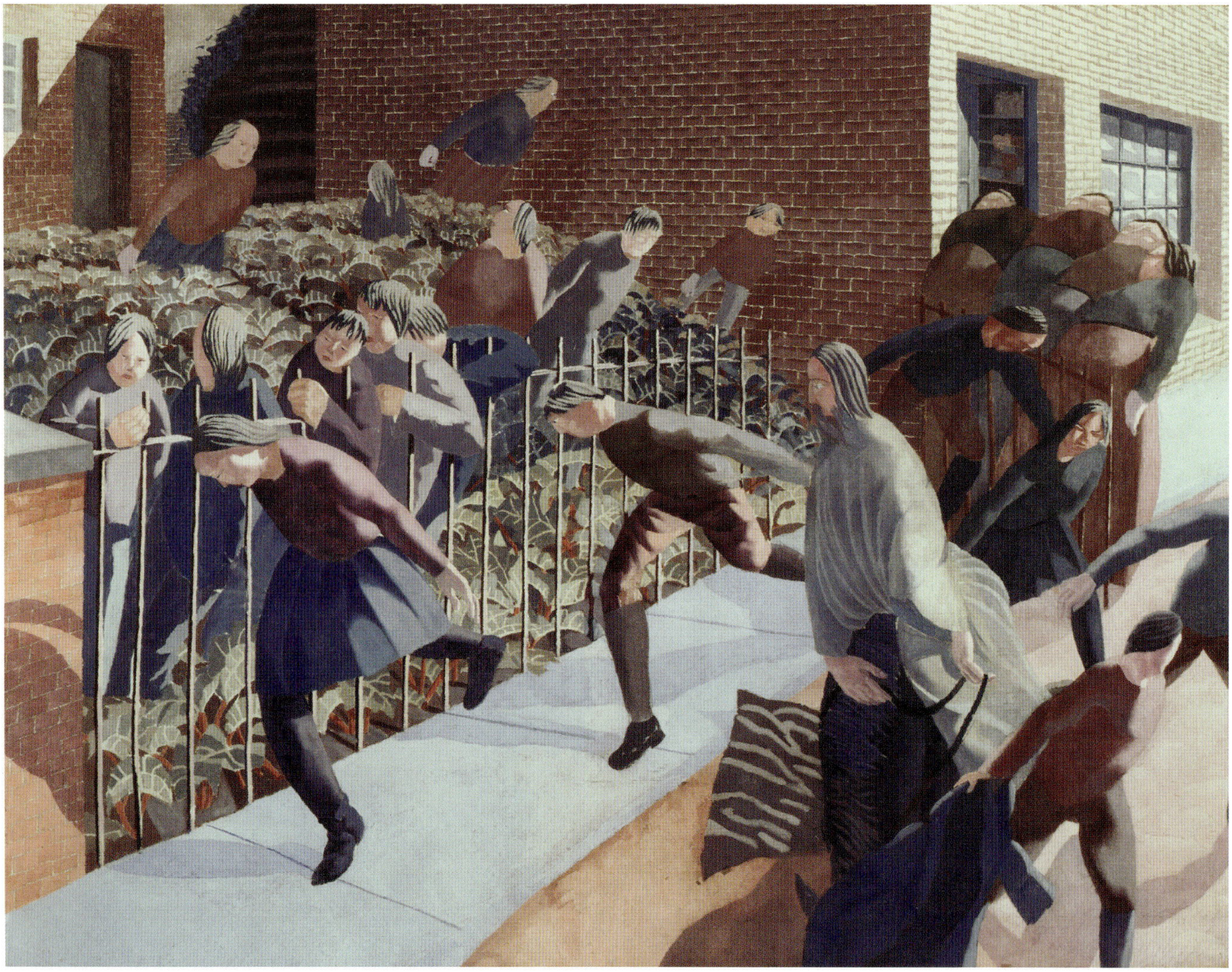

Christ's Entry into Jerusalem c1919

Stanley Spencer (1891–1959)

Oil on canvas 114.2 x 144.8cm
Bought by the Leeds Art Collections Fund 1941

One of six Spencer paintings bought during Philip Hendy's Directorship. Here the High Street in Cookham provides the Jerusalem background for Christ's arrival

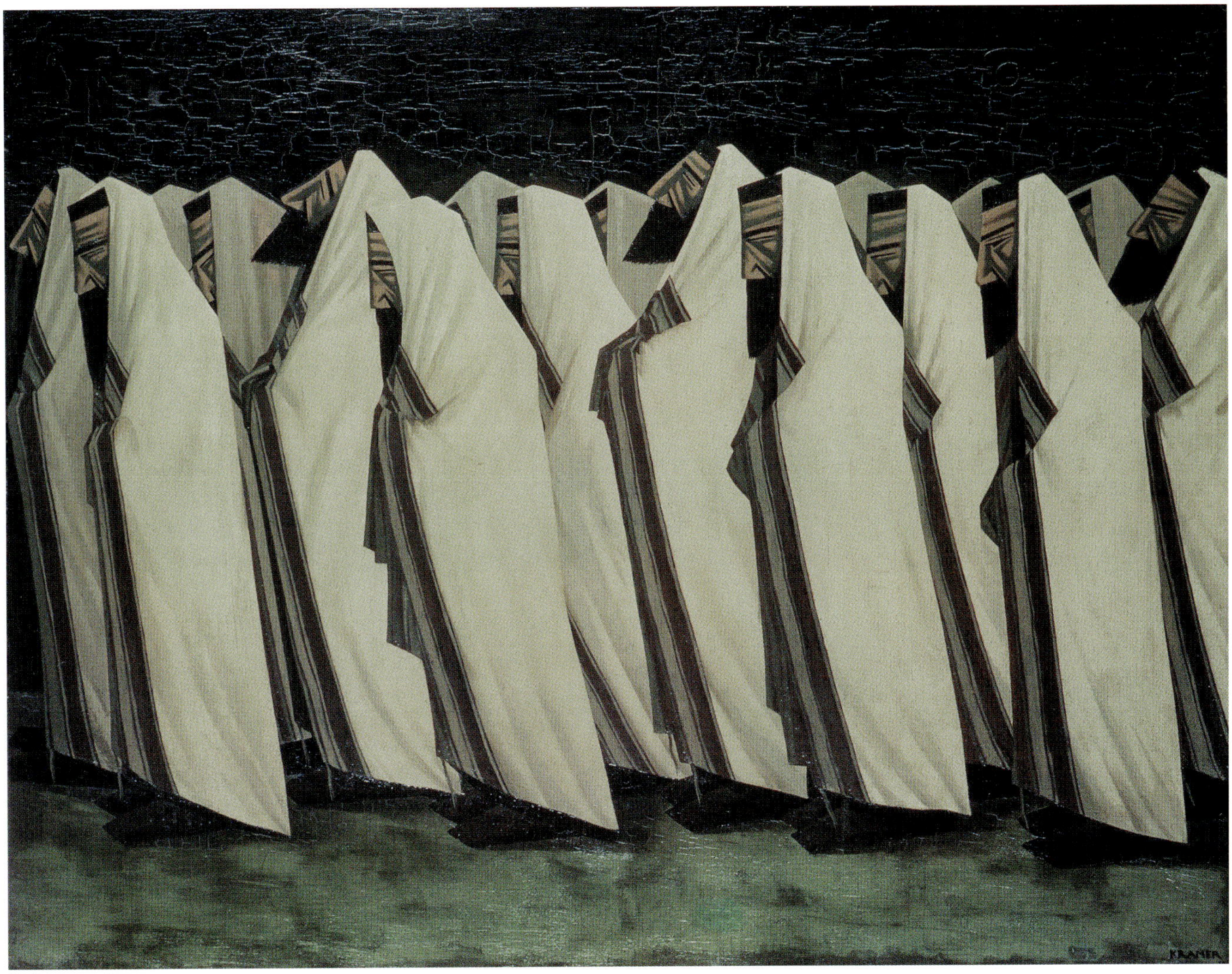

The Day of Atonement 1919

Jacob Kramer (1892–1962)

Oil on canvas 99 x 121.9cm
Given by the Leeds Jewish Community 1920

In this deeply moving procession of Jewish scholars wearing their prayer shawls, Kramer has reduced everything to the purest form, thus creating a hieratic frieze, like some ancient Assyrian relief

British Impressionism: The Sam Wilson Collection

Leeds woollen manufacturer, Sam Wilson (1857–1918) was singled out in the leading art magazine *The Studio* in 1916 as having formed a modern and progressive collection.

Deliberately avoiding the charms of the Royal Academy, with its continuing conservative bias, and focusing instead on 'English Impressionists' like Mark Senior, Wilson built up a collection of over three hundred paintings, sculptures, oriental porcelain and Gillow furniture, which he left to the City of Leeds in 1918. A sum of money was also bequeathed for the conversion of a warehouse at the back of the Art Gallery into a suitable gallery for his collection. This was completed in 1925; the walls hung with Fortuny wallpaper and the whole enterprise was opened by the French Ambassador on 12 October 1925.

Wilson had first shown his generosity in 1906, when he bought from the Venice Biennale Frank Brangwyn's series of scenes of industry for presentation to Leeds the following year. This set the tone for his purchases. Between 1900 and 1915 he spent about £9,000 on his collection, advised by artist Mark Senior as to suitable acquisitions. His favourites included Frank Brangwyn, Senior himself, Georg Sauter, William Orpen, George Clausen and John Buxton Knight.

A few less obvious artists were Henry Le Sidaner, Eugene Boudin, EA Hornel and Joaquin Sorolla y Bastida; Wilson's collection also included several sculptures by Leighton, Olsen and Gilbert. Most extraordinary was the fireplace designed by Alfred Gilbert, commissioned for Wilson's house, Rutland Lodge at Potternewton, Leeds.

Viewed from today's perspective the choices seem safe, well-painted and perhaps a little unadventurous. But it was a determined attempt to avoid the over-elaborate subject matter still to be found at the Royal Academy. If we do regret the absence of Monet, Renoir or Cézanne, we can admire the fresh charms of Clausen's *Little Girl* and Sauter's *Memories of Love*, the rugged heroism of Brangwyn's *The Blacksmiths*, and the surprising frankness of Orpen's *Nude*.

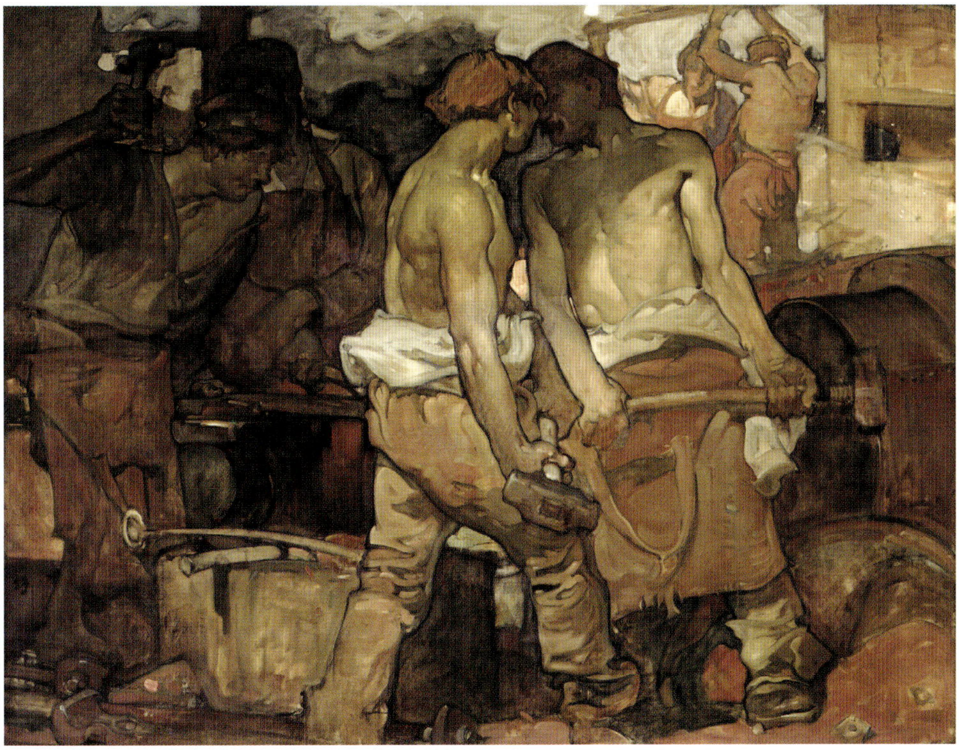

The Blacksmiths 1904–05
Sir Frank Brangwyn (1867–1956)
Oil on canvas 165.1 x 205.7cm
Given by Sam Wilson 1906

One of Wilson's most generous gifts, this series of five decorative panels celebrate British industry and the working man

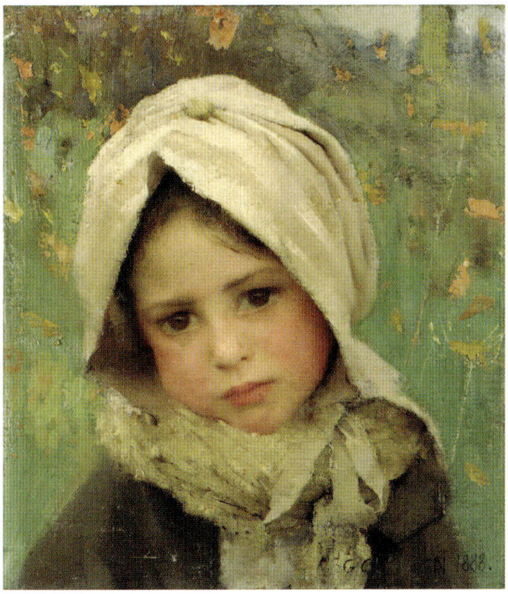

A Little Child 1888
Sir George Clausen (1852–1944)
Oil on canvas 35.6 x 30.5cm
Sam Wilson bequest 1918

An example of Clausen's early realism

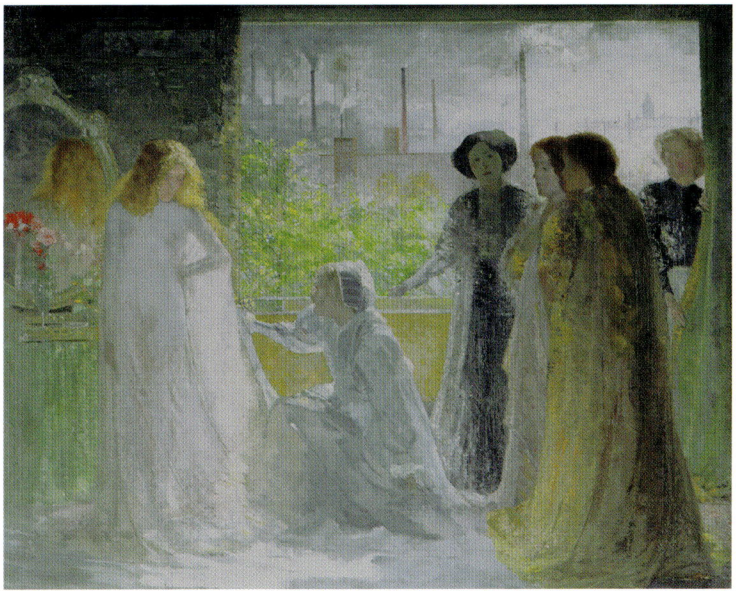

The Leeds Picture c1908
Georg Sauter (1866–1937)
Oil on canvas 104.1 x 129.5cm
Sam Wilson bequest 1918

Industrial Leeds forming a backdrop to an image of wealth and industry

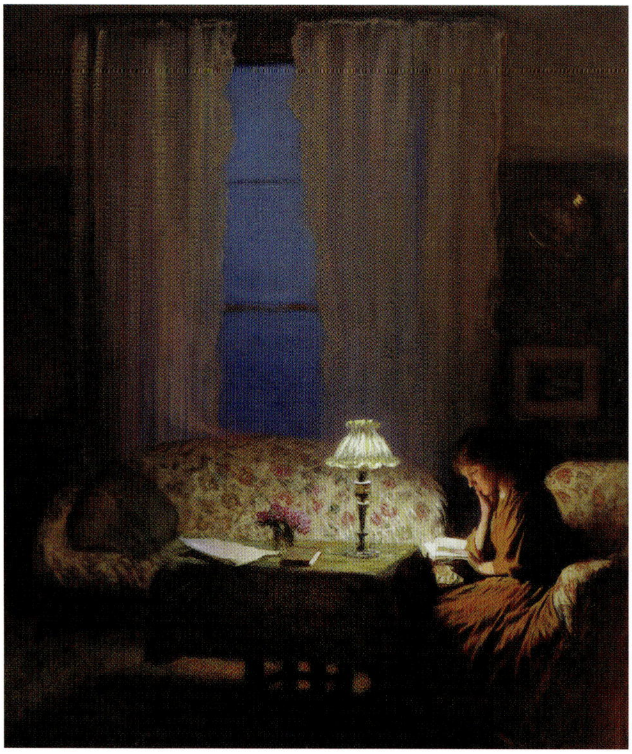

Reading by Lamplight 1909
Sir George Clausen (1852–1944)
Oil on canvas 73.2 x 58.4cm
Stanley Wilson bequest 1940

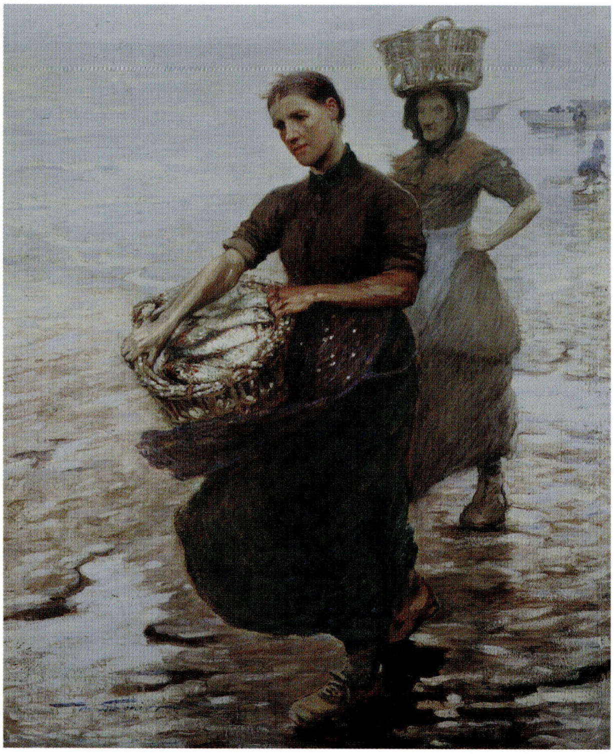

Toil c1901
Mark Senior (1864–1927)
Oil on canvas 127 x 101.6cm
Bought 1901

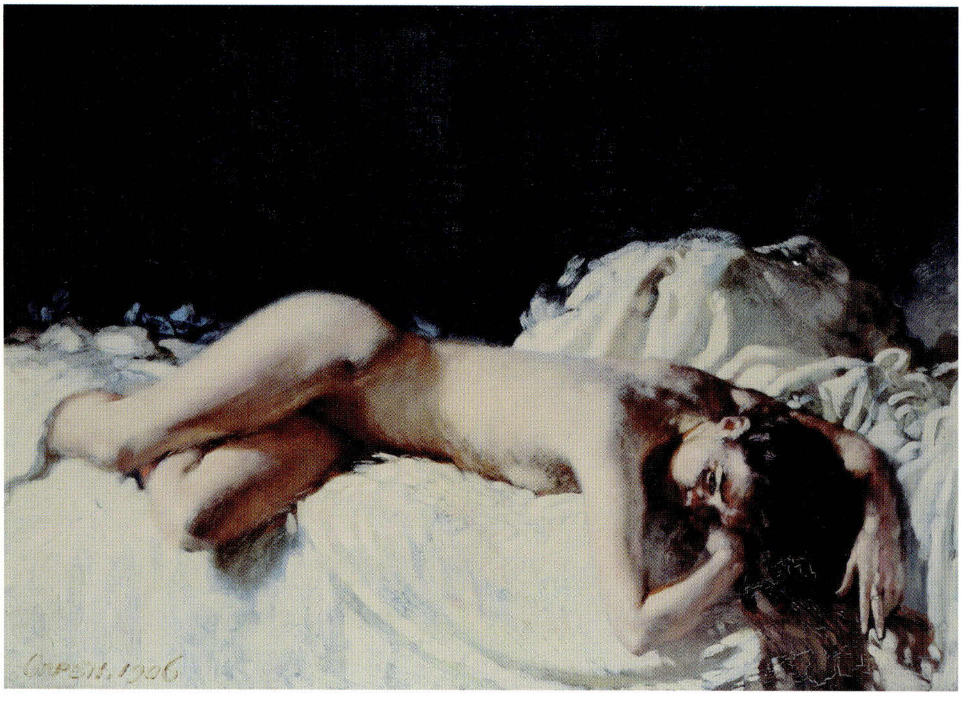

Nude Study 1906
Sir William Orpen (1878–1931)
Oil on canvas 56.5 x 81.3cm
Sam Wilson bequest 1918

A revealing painting by Orpen and a daring choice by Wilson

Silver Birches (Chemin de Bouleaux) c1912

Adriaan Josef Heymans (1839–1921) Oil on canvas 35.6 × 58.4cm Sam Wilson bequest 1918

A scene in the Ardennes

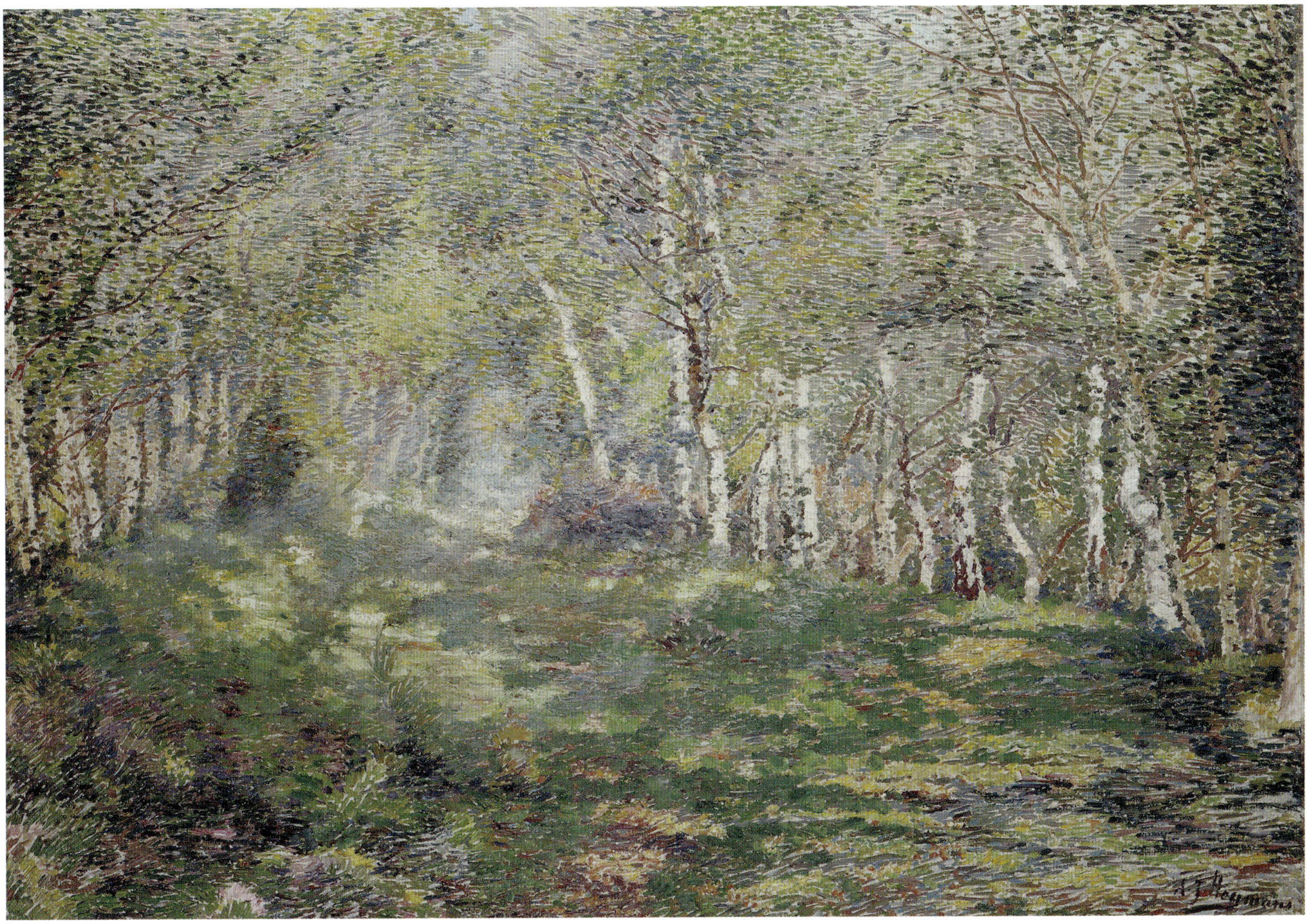

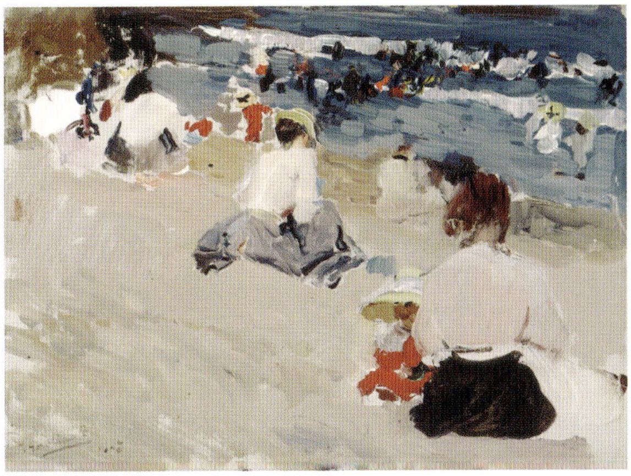

Ladies on the Beach 1906

Joaquin Sorolla y Bastida (1863–1923)

Oil on board 15.9 × 22.2cm
Sam Wilson bequest 1918

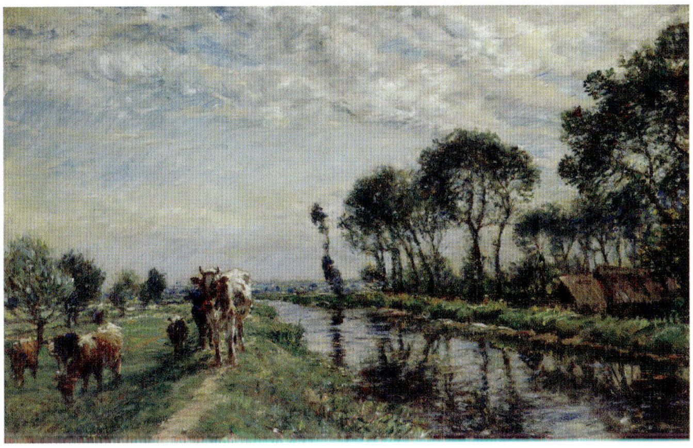

The Waterways c1906

Mark Fisher (1841–1923)

Oil on canvas 35.6 × 53.2cm
Sam Wilson bequest 1918

Modernism: Painting in Britain 1920–1950

Following the departure of Curator Frank Rutter to the Admiralty in 1917, and the removal of the Gallery collections for safe keeping during the First World War, there seemed little chance to acquire advanced art of the day. Psychologically the war exerted a profound effect on artists in the immediate aftermath of fighting, so the 1920s began in a subdued mood.

Solomon Kaines Smith became Curator of the Art Gallery in 1924, (which had been administered by the City Librarian in the interim), to be renamed Director in 1925. From 1927 to 1931 Frank Lambert brought about a much-needed facelift to the building and even the chance to see some modern art, including Jacob Epstein's *Genesis* exhibited in 1931. Lambert was followed by John Rothenstein until 1933. However, it was in the following years that a significant rise in the profile of the Gallery's modern collection took place, masterminded by Philip Hendy who stayed until 1945.

It is no exaggeration to say that, of all the Gallery Directors since George Birkett, Hendy made the most significant impact on the oil paintings collection. He set out to build up a modern collection, featuring mostly British artists from the turn of the century, up to his time. Remarkably, he persuaded the Town Council to provide an annual purchase grant fund from 1937, continued ever since.

Hendy's collecting for Leeds included eleven Walter Sickerts, six Matthew Smiths, five Stanley Spencers and six paintings by Edward Wadsworth. Works by most other leading British artists of the period were bought and, during the 1939–1945 war, a pioneering series of exhibitions was held at Temple Newsam, Leeds, featuring emerging 'new' artists such as Henry Moore, Paul Nash, Ben Nicholson and Augustus John, thus establishing the reputation of Leeds as a centre for contemporary art.

Directors who followed Hendy added to the list of achievements but not on quite his scale. Several Impressionist and related paintings by Sisley and Hayden joined the Derain, and efforts to represent Camden Town artists Ginner, Gilman and Gore were successful. Important war-time paintings were distributed in 1947 by the War Artists' Advisory Committee, which gave to the city paintings and drawings by many leading artists including Henry Moore and Graham Sutherland.

As the Gallery collections had mostly been evacuated to Temple Newsam during the war, the main emphasis in 1947 was on re-opening the building to incorporate a new front door onto the street, giving access to Victoria Gardens. While the proposed new Library, Museum and Art Gallery complex of 1937 was halted by the war, at least the collections could now be said to be worthy of a visit (a fact noted by Leeds artist Jacob Kramer).

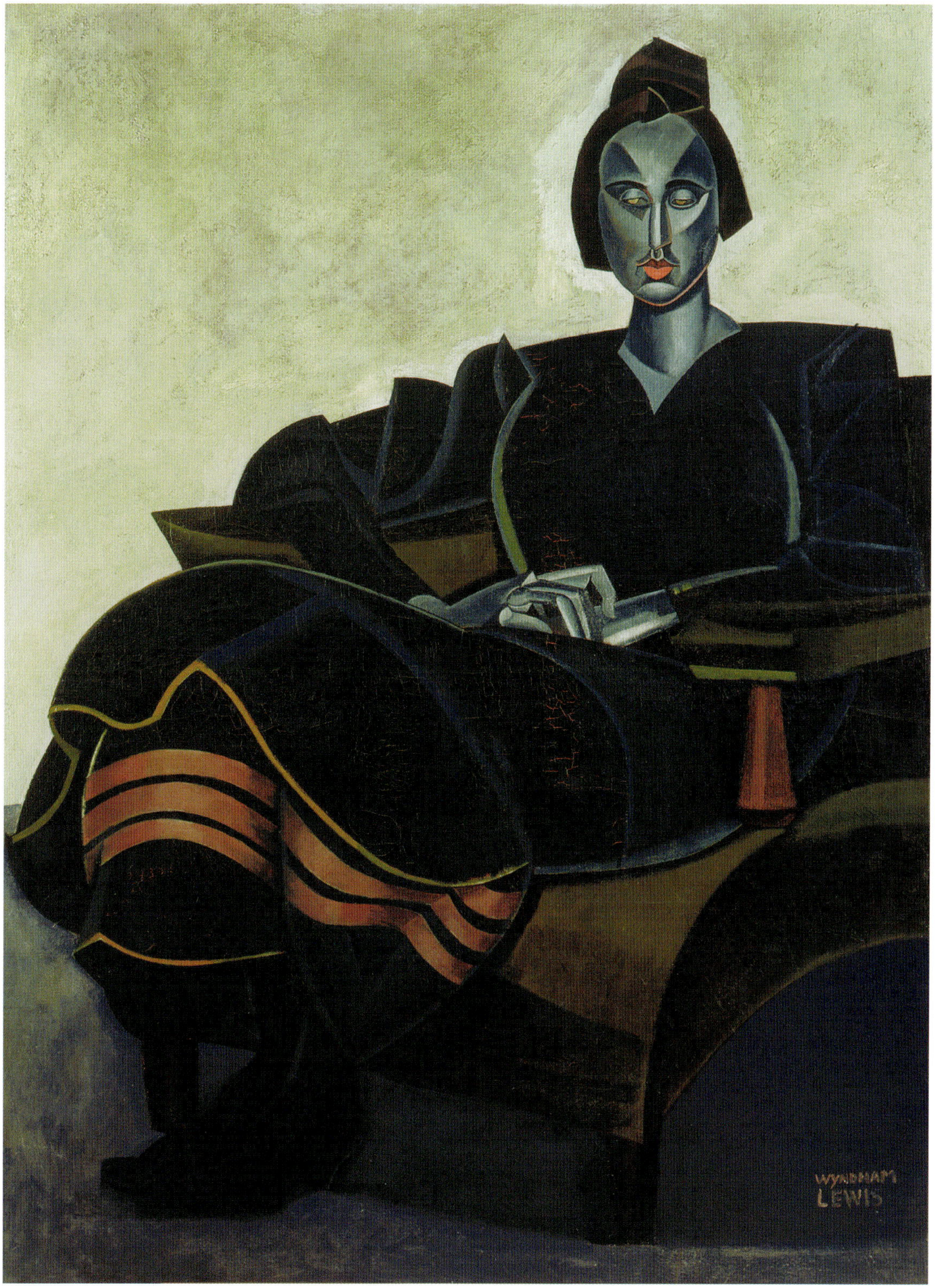

Praxitella c1921

Percy Wyndham Lewis (1882–1957)

Oil on canvas 142.2 x 101.6cm Given by Edward Wadsworth through the Contemporary Art Society 1945

This portrait in the Vorticist style features Iris Barry in cubistic form, creating a sinister figure as a kind of robotic female Praxiteles

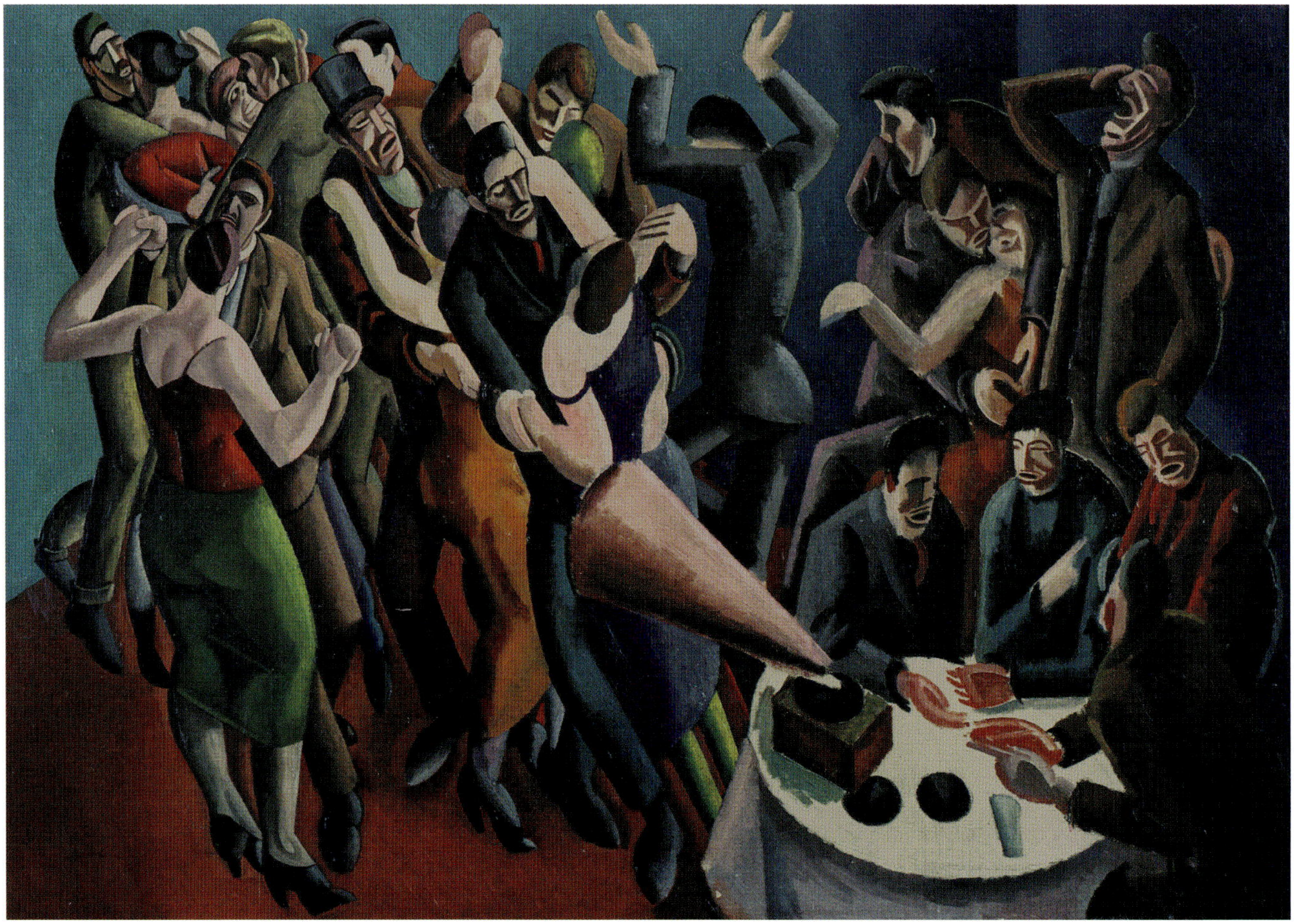

ABOVE

The Dance Club 1923

William Roberts (1895–1980)

Oil on canvas 76.2 x 106.6cm

Given by the Contemporary Art Society 1928

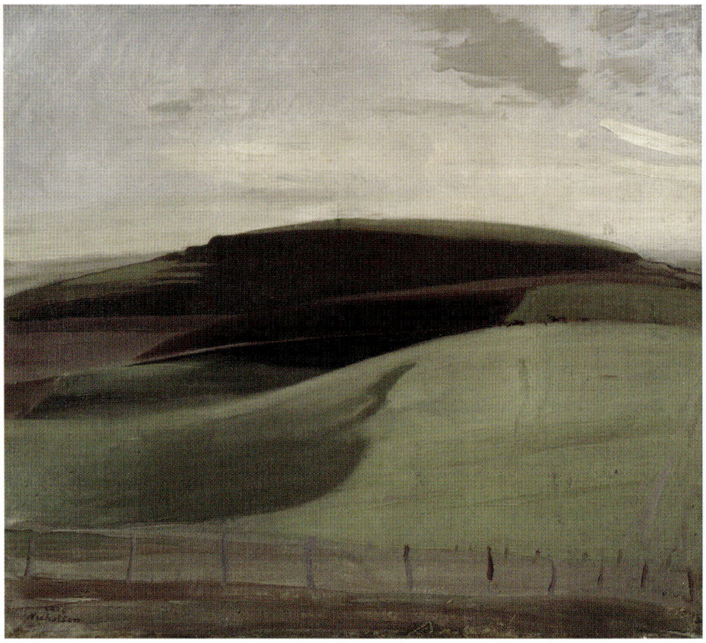

On the Downs 1924

William Nicholson (1872–1949)

Oil on canvas 53.2 x 59.8cm

Herbert Hepworth bequest 1943

Sunrise Between the Hedges 1939

Graham Sutherland (1903–1980) Oil on canvas 54.6 x 90.2cm Bought 1941

Although not strictly surrealist, Sutherland often creates landscapes and plant forms with strange anthropomorphic qualities

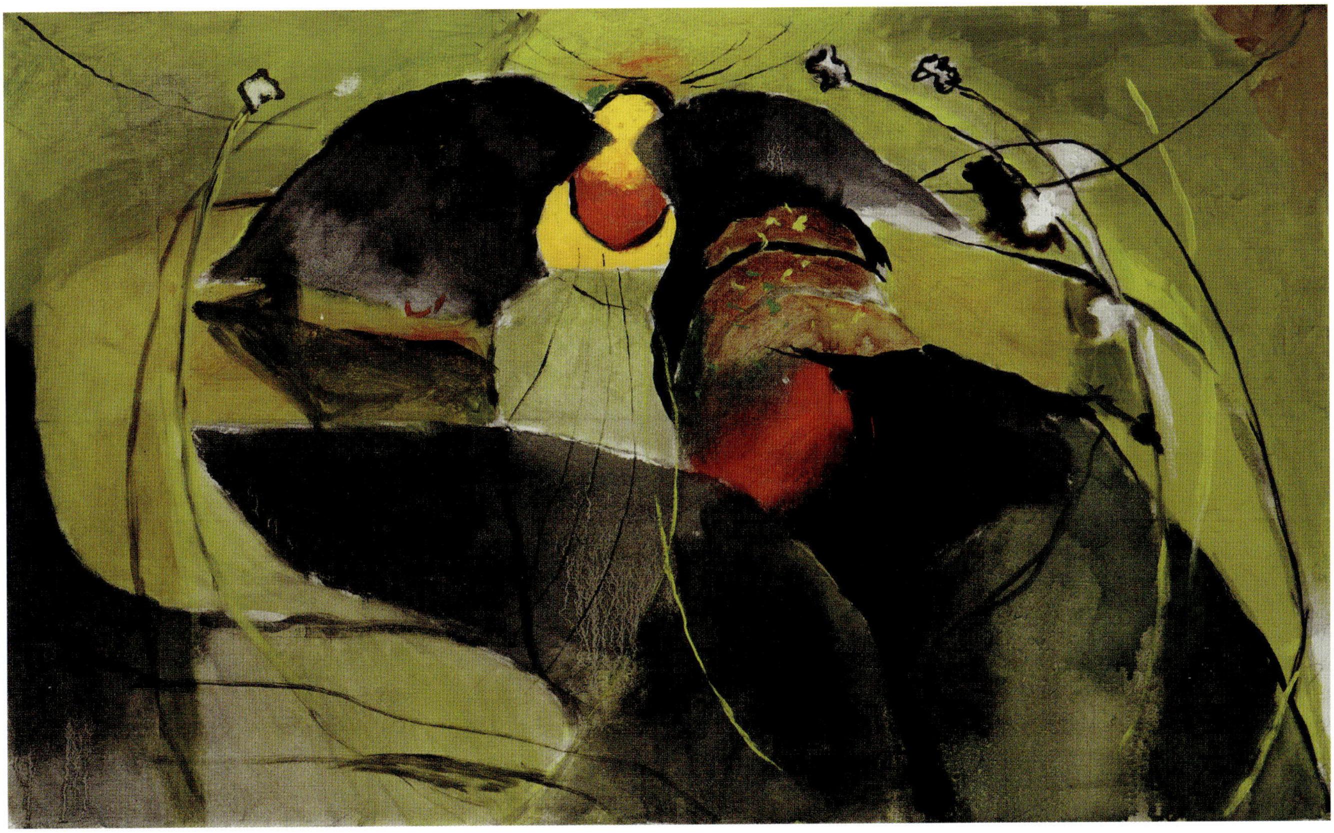

Hazel Wood 1944

Ivon Hitchens (1893–1979)

Oil on canvas 55.8 x 149.8cm
Bought 1945

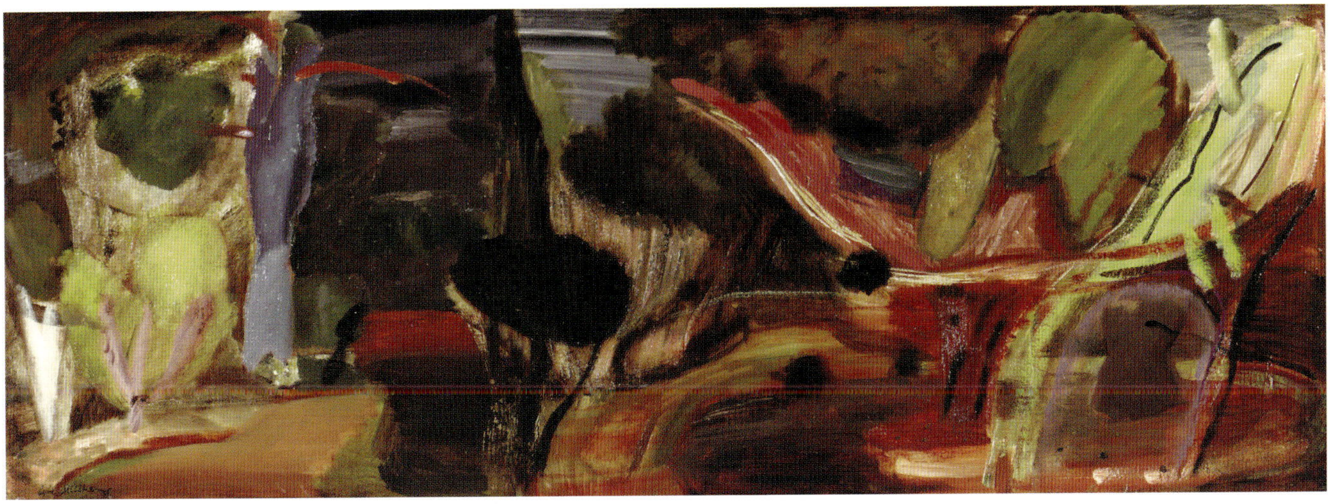

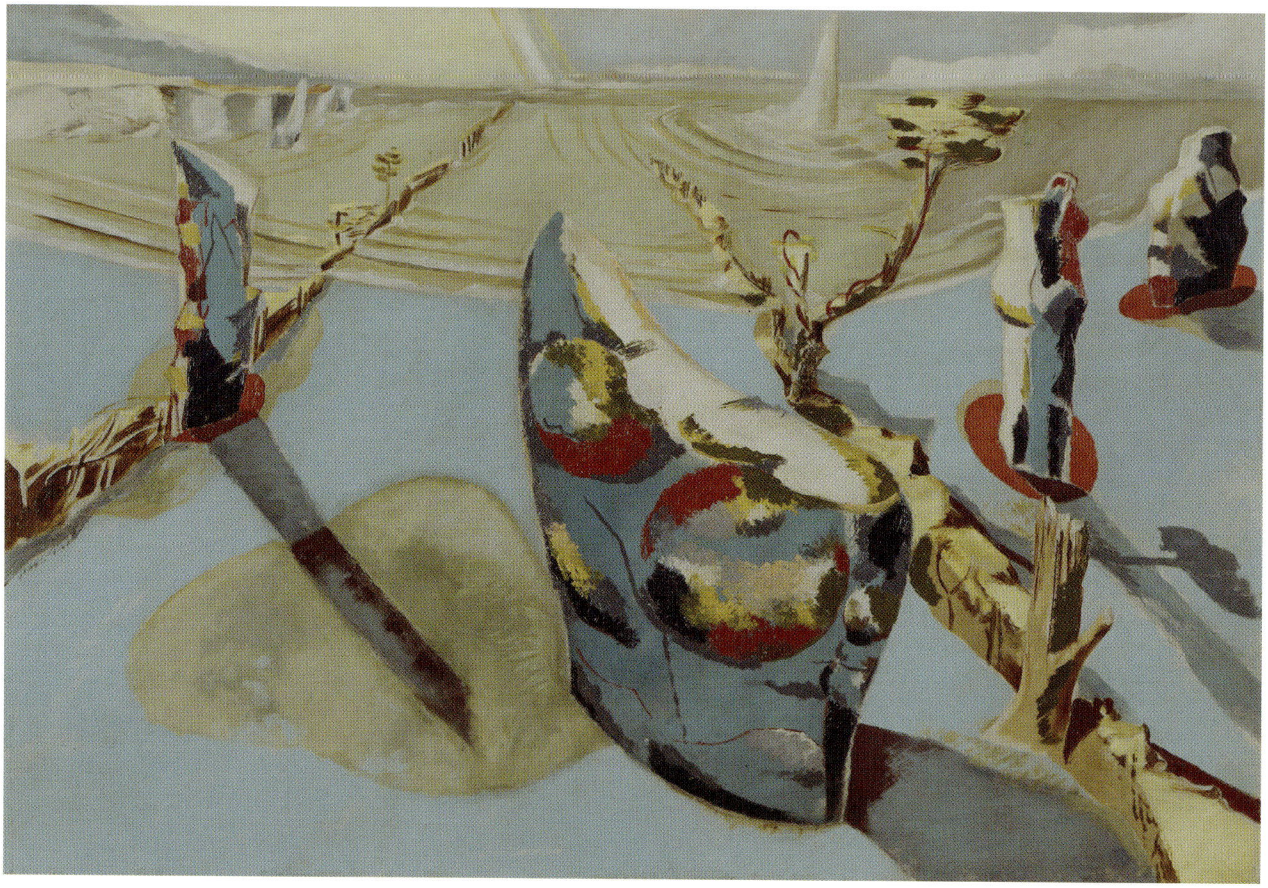

Circle of the Monoliths c1938
Paul Nash (1889–1946)
Oil on canvas 78.8 x 104.1cm Bought 1950
Here Nash combines the stone circle at Avebury, Wiltshire with the sea at Swanage in a dream image

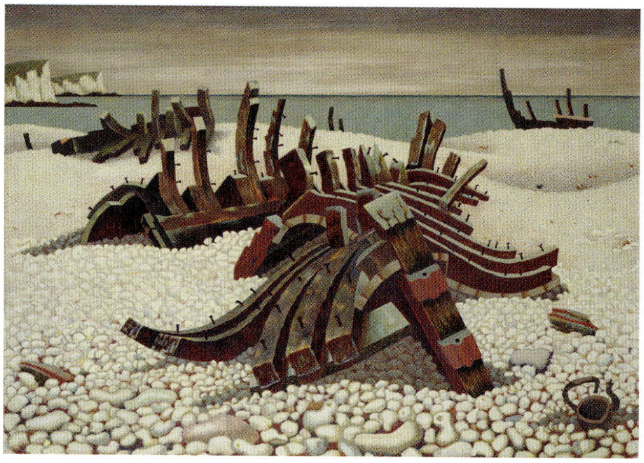

Requiescat 1940
Edward Wadsworth (1889–1949)
Tempera on wood 63.3 x 86.3cm
Bought 1941

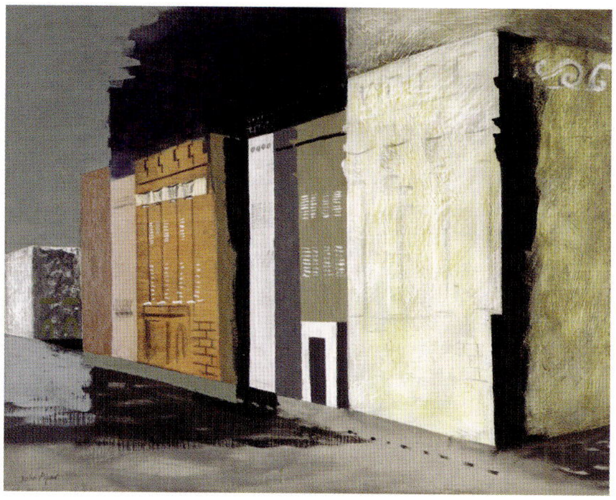

Dead Resort, Kempton c1939
John Piper (1903–1992)
Oil on canvas on board 45.7 x 55.8cm
Given by the Contemporary Art Society 1941

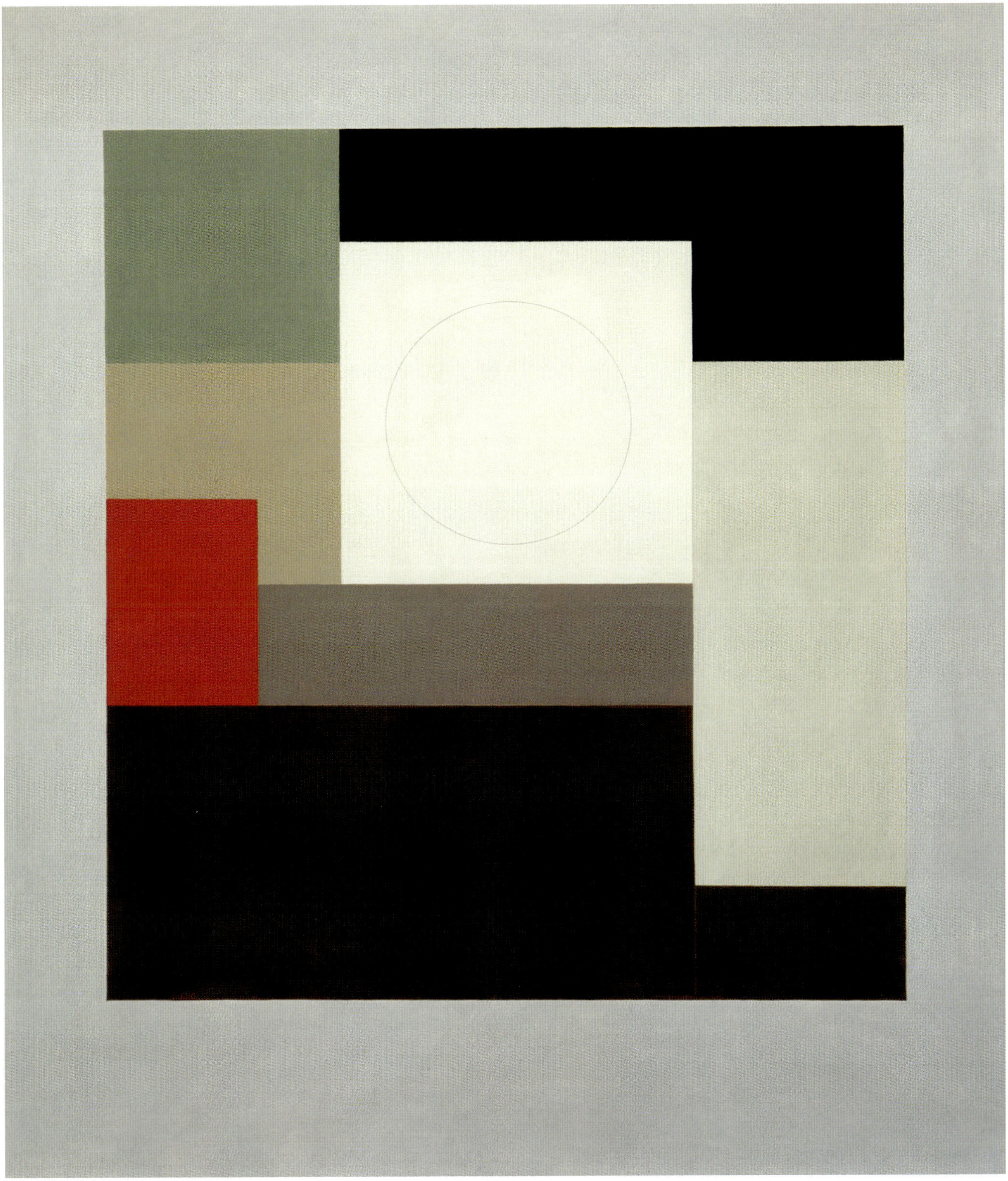

Painting 1940

Ben Nicholson (1894–1982)

Gouache on board 60.9 × 53.2cm
Bought 1945

Post-War British Art 1950–1980

The most controversial painting (at least for the members) bought by the 'Friends', the Leeds Art Collections Fund, turned out to be Francis Bacon's *Painting* 1950, a mysterious study of a male figure. It now appears a 'classic' Bacon.

The Gallery building itself was about to see a series of changes which lasted until the 1980s. As well as the new front door, improvements internally meant a new floor over the centre court, creating a lecture theatre and first floor gallery, with a picture store below. In 1950 the Gregory Fellowships (residencies) at Leeds University were founded by EC (Peter) Gregory, a Director of Lund Humphries, enabling young artists, sculptors, poets and musicians to work in Leeds.

Exhibitions usually followed the residency and the opportunity to buy examples by the artists became available. In this way the Gallery acquired significant pieces by Terry Frost, Alan Davie, Hubert Dalwood, Reg Butler, Kenneth Armitage, Trevor Bell, Austin Wright, Norman Stevens, Ainslie Yule, John Walker, Keith Milow and Sergei Prokofiev.

During the 1950s there was strong support from the Leeds Art Collections Fund to buy sculpture so that, by 1958, a dedicated Sculpture Gallery was created and in 1965 the Fund bought Henry Moore's *Three Piece Reclining Figure no. 2 Bridge Prop*. This development of the sculpture collection was to lead eventually to the establishment of a new gallery dedicated to sculpture, added onto the front of the building, and to the Henry Moore Centre for the Study of Sculpture, opened in 1982, later moving next door to the Henry Moore Institute, opened in 1993.

However, the earlier buying policy of Philip Hendy, particularly in acquiring oil paintings, could not be maintained, especially with the development of the collections of decorative art at Temple Newsam House and Lotherton Hall. Post-war movements such as Neo-Romanticism and the St Ives School were poorly represented, as was the 'Kitchen Sink' group of the 1950s. The international rebirth of British art following the emergence of 'Pop Art' in the swinging London of the 1960s was represented usually by prints and some sculpture. However, there were several important purchases of more abstract work by artists including Robyn Denny, Mark Lancaster and John Walker.

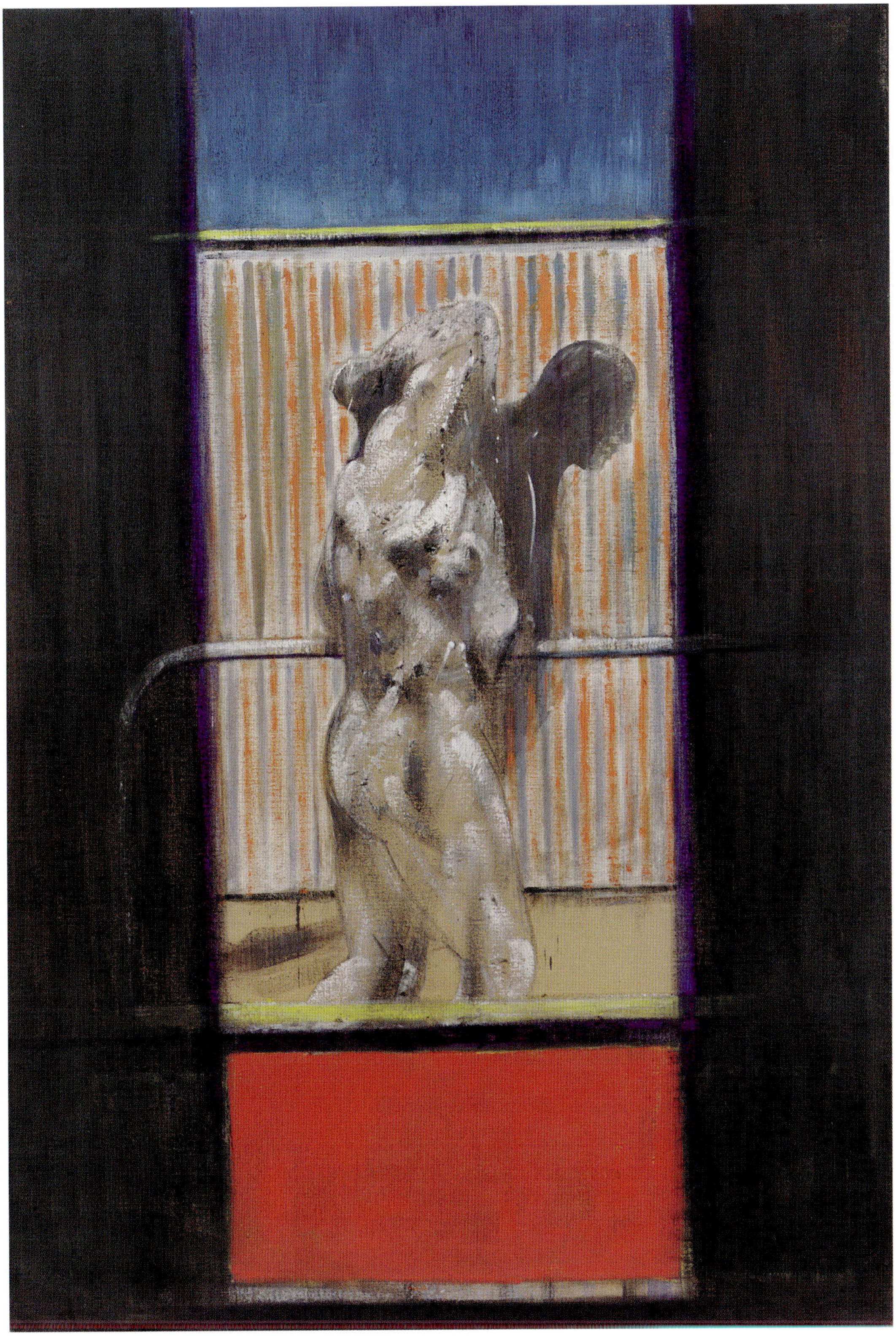

Painting 1950

Francis Bacon (1909–1992)

Oil on canvas 198.1 x 132.1cm
Bought by the Leeds Art Collections Fund 1951

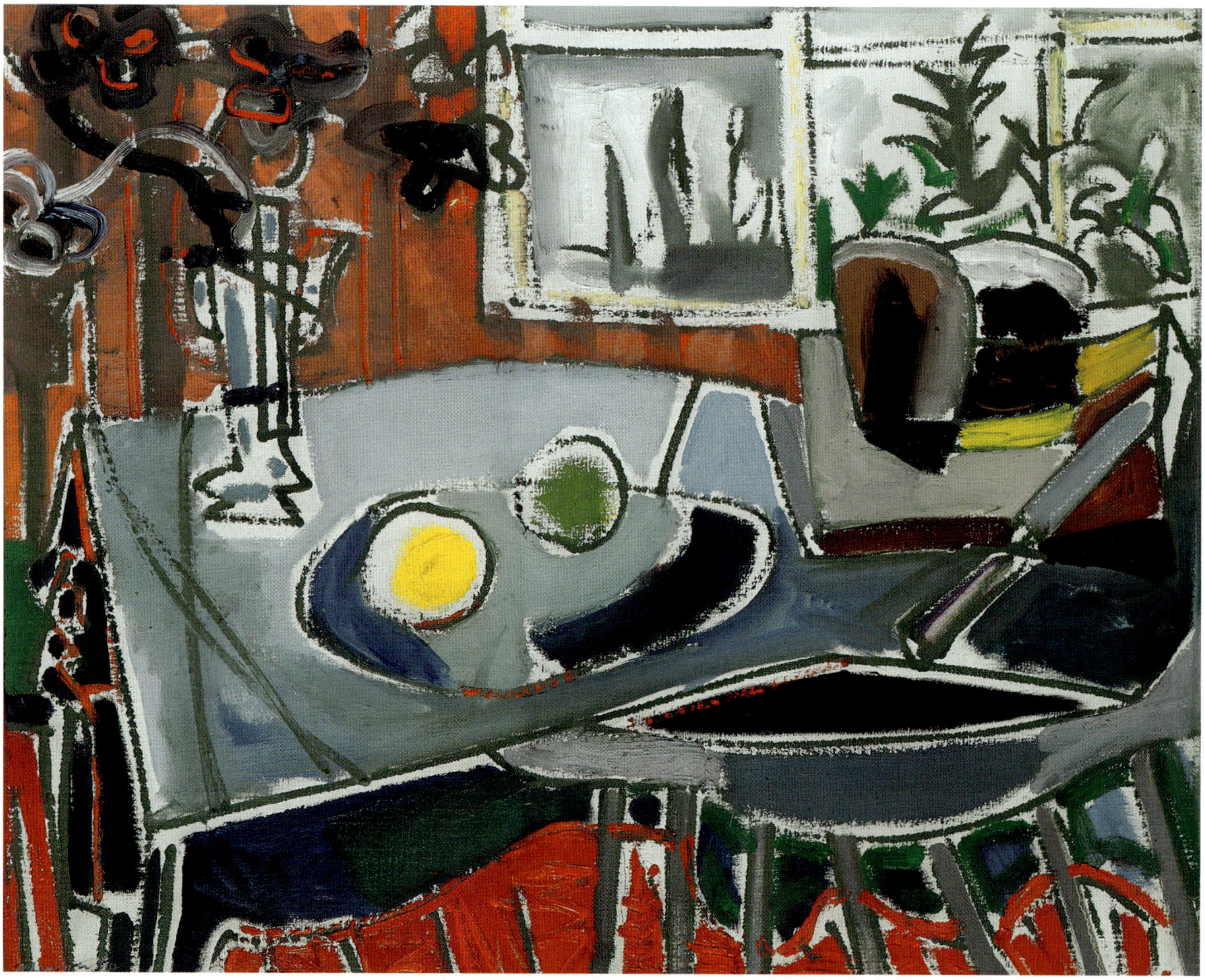

ABOVE

Anemones and Lemons 1950

Patrick Heron (1920–1999)

Oil on canvas 51 x 61cm
Bought by the Leeds Art Collections Fund 1951

RIGHT

The Deposition of Christ 1958

Ceri Richards (1930–1971)

Oil on canvas 60.9 x 91.4cm
Bought by the Leeds Art Collections Fund 1958

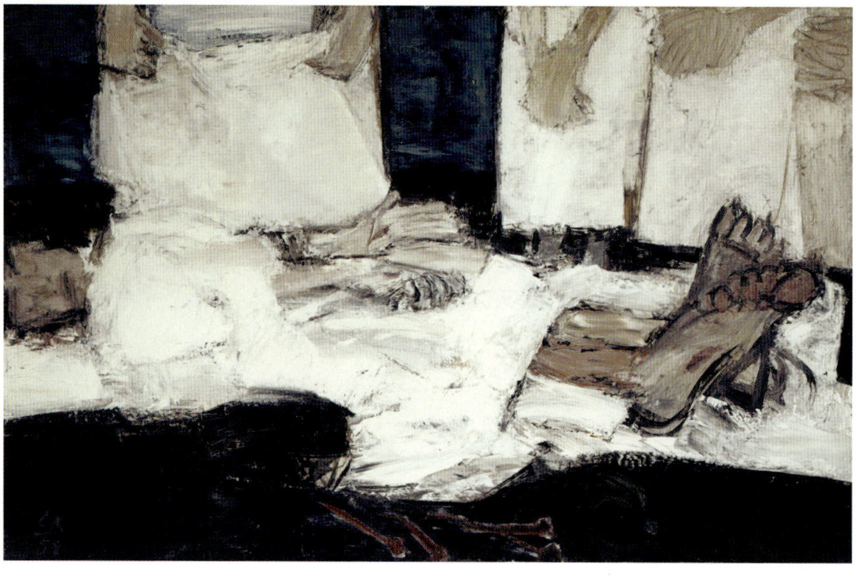

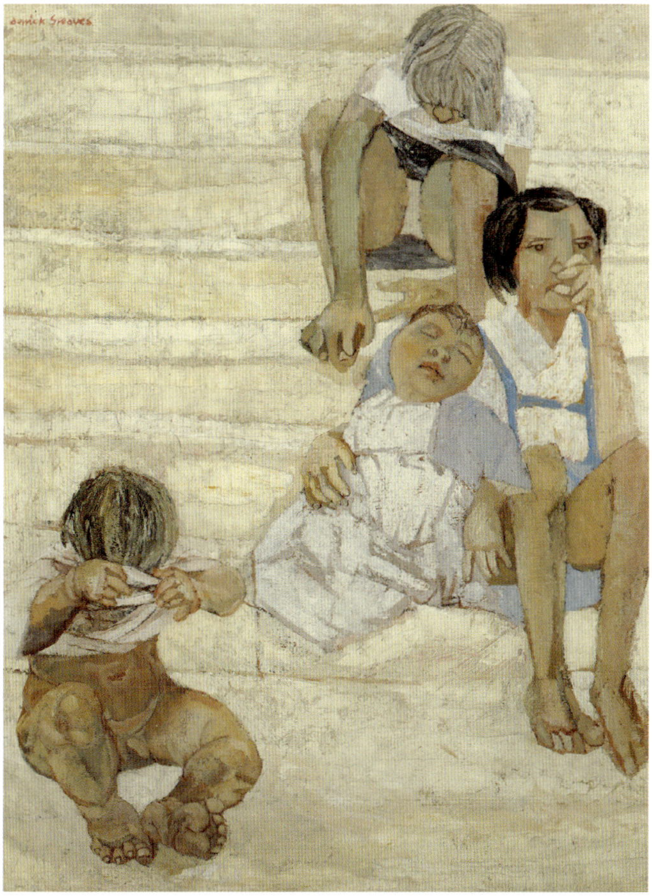

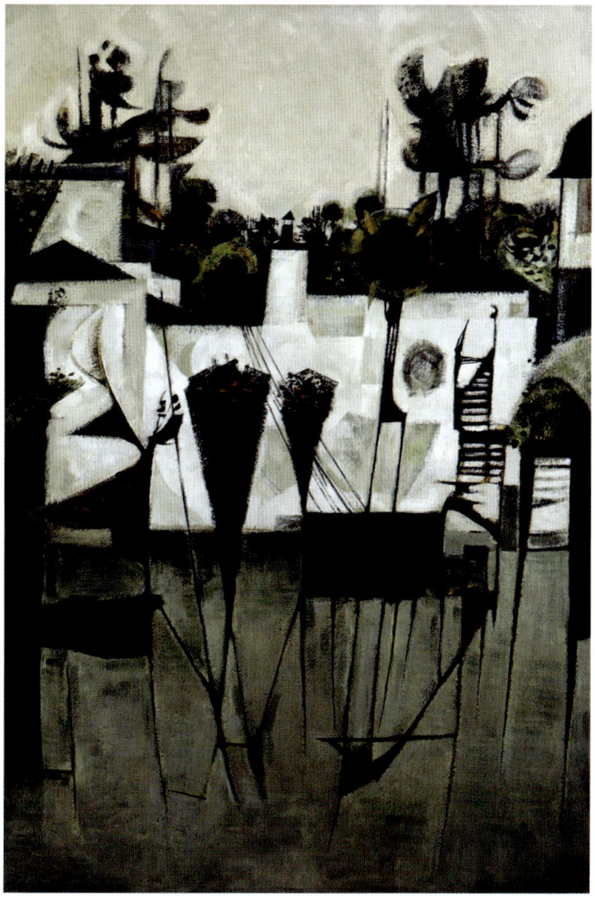

ABOVE LEFT

Children on Steps c1956

Derrick Greaves (born 1927)

Oil on canvas 121.9 x 91.4cm
Bought 1956

ABOVE RIGHT

Outbuildings Pastorale 1952

Alan Reynolds (born 1926)

Oil on canvas 144.8 x 94cm
Given by the Contemporary Art Society 1956

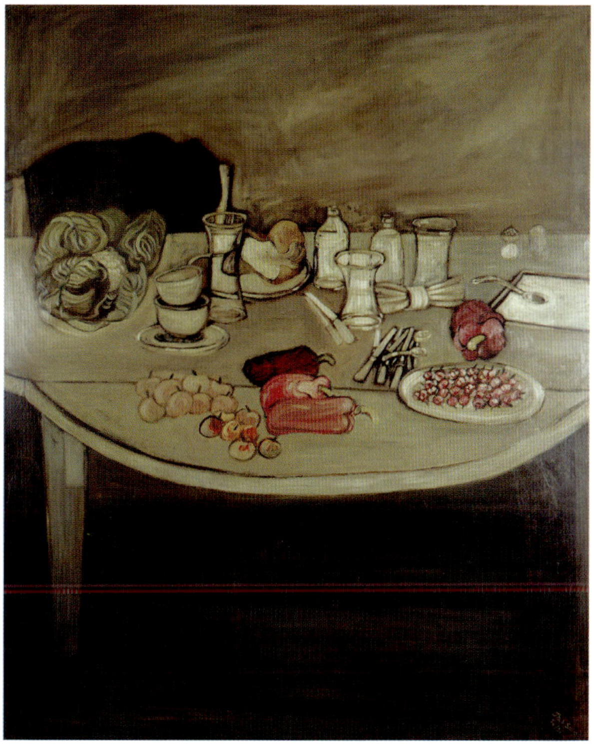

Still Life with Bowl of Cherries 1954–55

Jack Smith (born 1928)

Oil on board 172.8 x 121.9cm
Bought with the aid of grants from V&A Purchase Grant Fund and the Leeds Art Collections Fund in memory of WT Oliver 1991

In the Face of the Witch 1955

Alan Davie (born 1920)

Oil on board 99.7 x 116.8cm
Given by the Contemporary Art Society 1962

Davie was Gregory Fellow at the University of Leeds from 1956 to 1959. His abstract canvases contain strange symbols with surrealist undertones

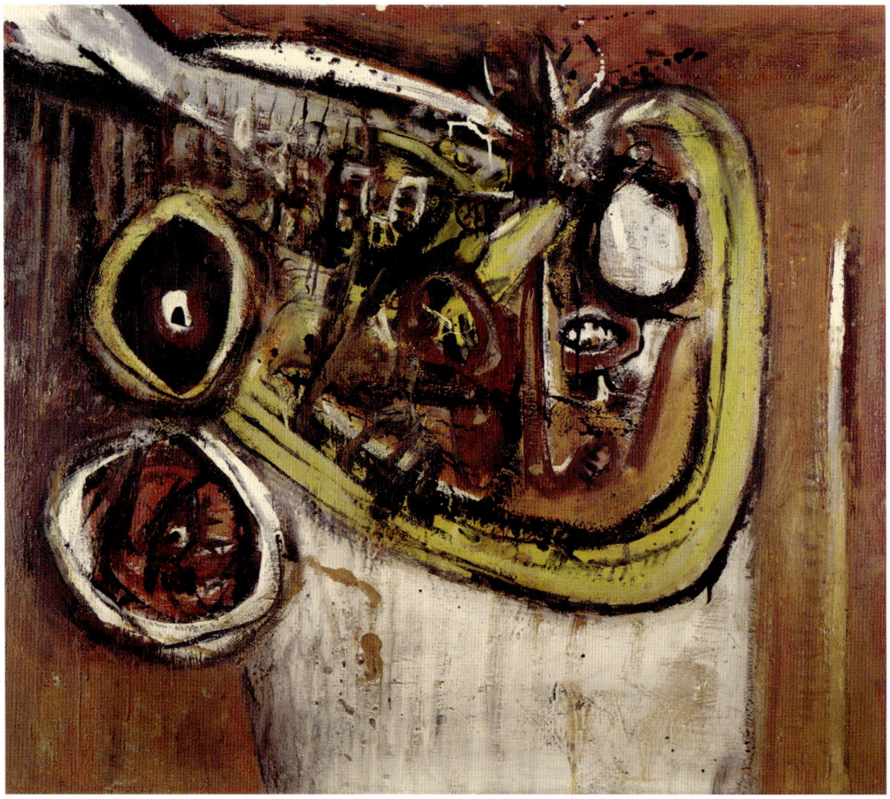

Maples Demolition, Euston Road 1960

Frank Auerbach (born 1931)

Oil on board 148.6 x 153.7cm
Given by the Contemporary Art Society 1965

Auerbach's expressionist technique is used to portray the changing face of London

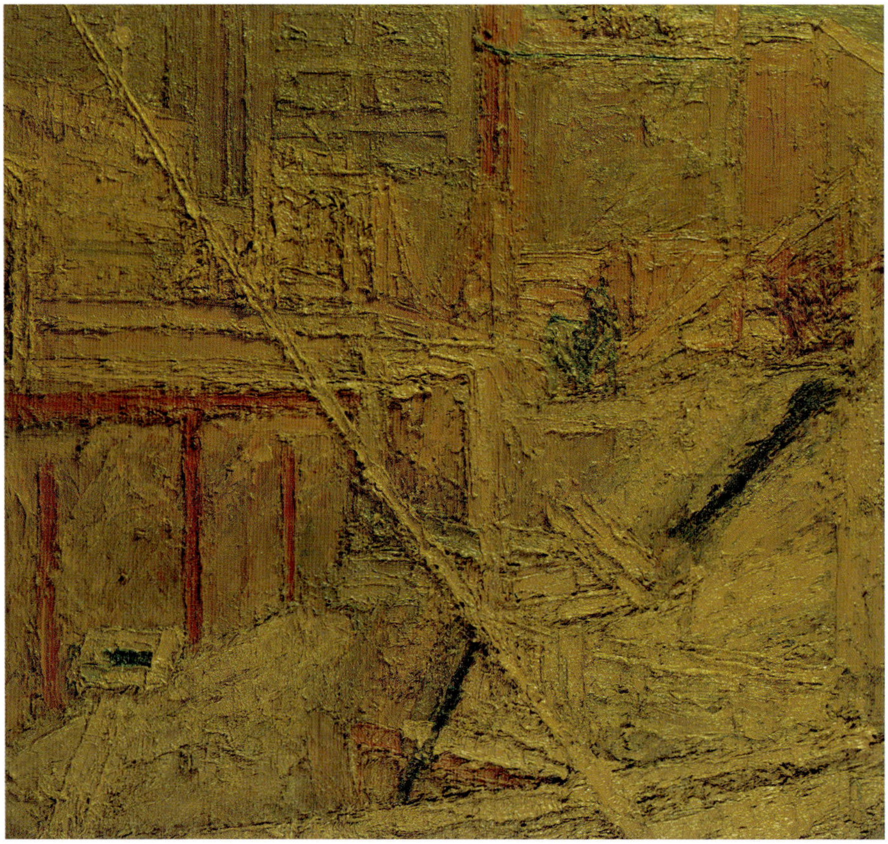

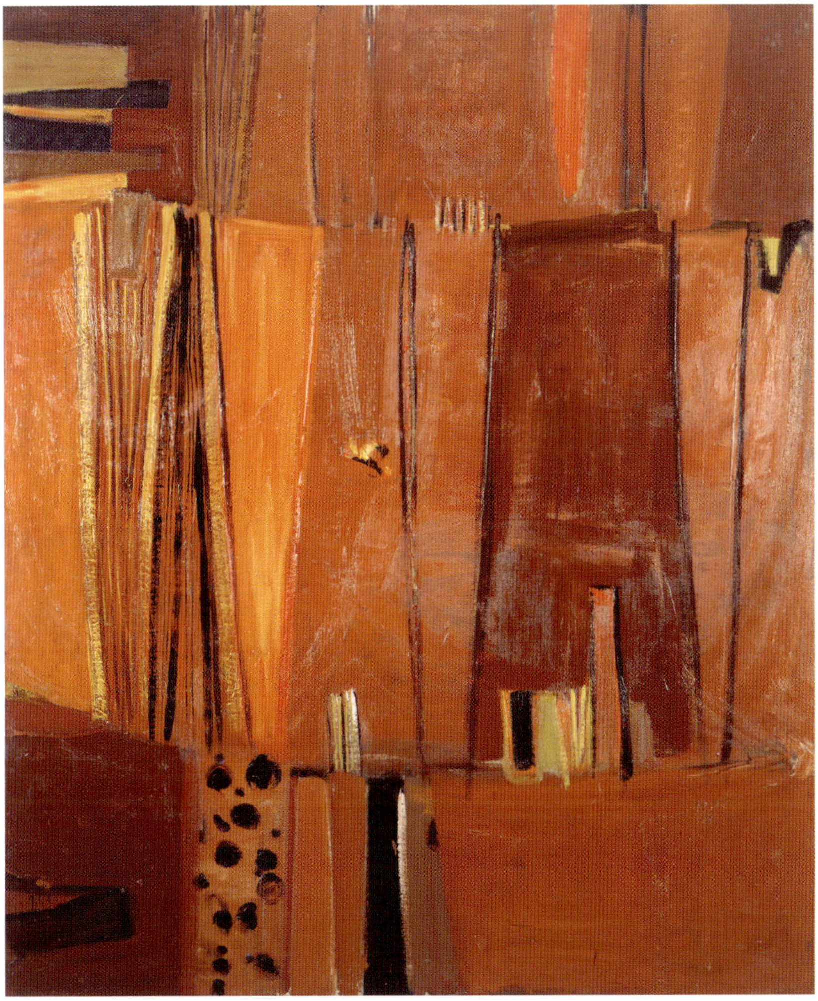

Brown Verticals c1958–59

Terry Frost (1915–2003)

Oil on canvas 213.4 x 171.8cm
Bought 1960

Frost was Gregory Fellow at the University of Leeds from 1954 to 1956. The rugged Yorkshire landscape provided inspiration for his work at the time

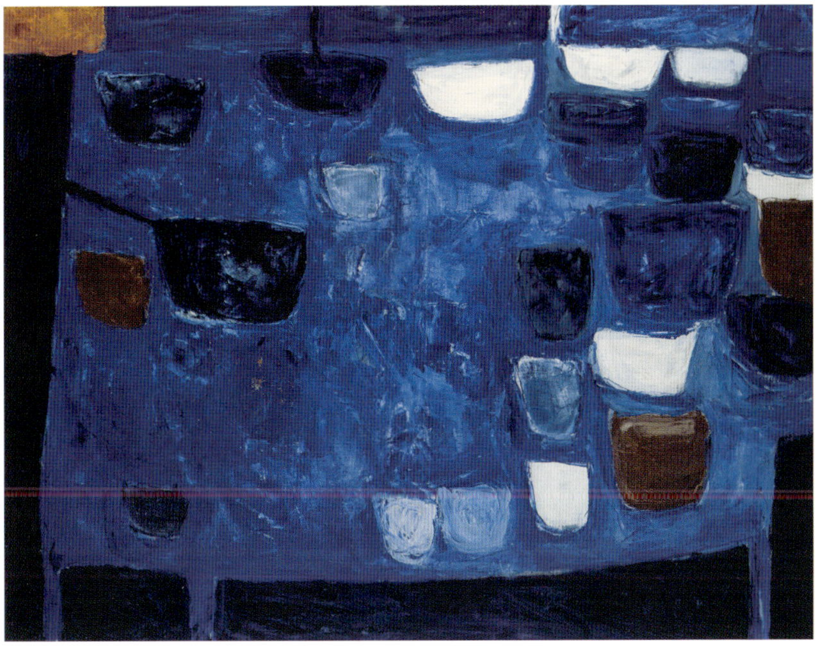

Blue Still Life c1957

William Scott (1913–1989)

Oil on canvas 106.6 x 132.1cm
Given by the Contemporary Art Society 1959

New Directions: Art Post-1980

Today, a hundred years after its establishment, the dominant medium represented in the Gallery is painting. The Gallery continues to develop the collection in this area, representing work by living artists just as the first Curators of the Gallery did, but these new works reflect current concerns.

From the beginning of the 20TH century painting itself has been challenged as the dominant medium for art – as, for instance, when Picasso and Braque began to use collage and add household materials to their paint. Stephen Willats draws this idea into the contemporary world with *Doppelgänger*, a work that incorporates a real shoe, tie, brick and empty can of lager.

Increasingly artists have seen new media as an attractive proposition, while major exhibitions such as *Unbound – Possibilities in Painting* at the Hayward Gallery in 1994 have continued to assert the viability of painting. From this show the Gallery purchased *The Artist in her Studio* by Paula Rego. Unlike the narrative paintings of the Victorian era, whose meaning can be easily accessed and researched, Rego in post-modern mode teases the viewer with a figurative work that suggests a narrative, but one that is hard to grasp, leaving meaning in a state of flux and dependent on meaning ascribed to it by the viewer.

Notable in recent acquisitions is the number of works by women artists such as Gillian Ayres, whose expressive essay in abstraction, *Helios,* entered the collection in 1991. At the end of the 19TH century a number of women artists were represented in the collection. Later, however, these paintings were considered unfashionable and, sadly, in 1937 some were even disposed of. During the rise of the Feminist movement in the 1970s very few works by women were acquired.

In 1999 Leeds embarked on the Special Collection Scheme. Supported by the Contemporary Art Society and funded by the Arts Council, this allowed the curatorial staff to develop the collections in new directions in line with the work being produced by students and tutors in the local universities.

Threshold to the Kingdom by Mark Wallinger was commissioned as part of the Holy Year celebrations in 2000. The video shows people entering the country in the arrivals hall of City Airport in London and the footage unfurls to the sublime *Miserere* by Allegri, composed for the choir of the Sistine Chapel.

Increasingly artists have come to question whether art requires a physical image or whether the visual can be suggested through other senses. The Special Collections Scheme has allowed the Gallery to commission American artist Bill Fontana to create a sound sculpture for Leeds; playing with the idea that sound has a three-dimensional character, in that it occupies a physical space. Fontana captured four sounds from the region and placed them around the Gallery and on the façade: the water in the Dark Arches; the wind turbines at Chelker Reservoir; the low seismic rumblings relayed from buried transmitters around Yorkshire, which make the sound of the waves beating against the Yorkshire coast audible; as well as the ticking of the Town Hall clock. Fontana has written of the Town Hall clock... *'it has been going since 1858 just think what transformations in our world have taken place in the intervening years. A visit to Leeds City Art Gallery gives us a chance to reflect on the world in which we live and our experiences of living...'*

Helios 1990

Gillian Ayres (born 1930)

Oil on canvas 152 x 152cm
Bought with the aid of a grant
from The Art Fund 1991

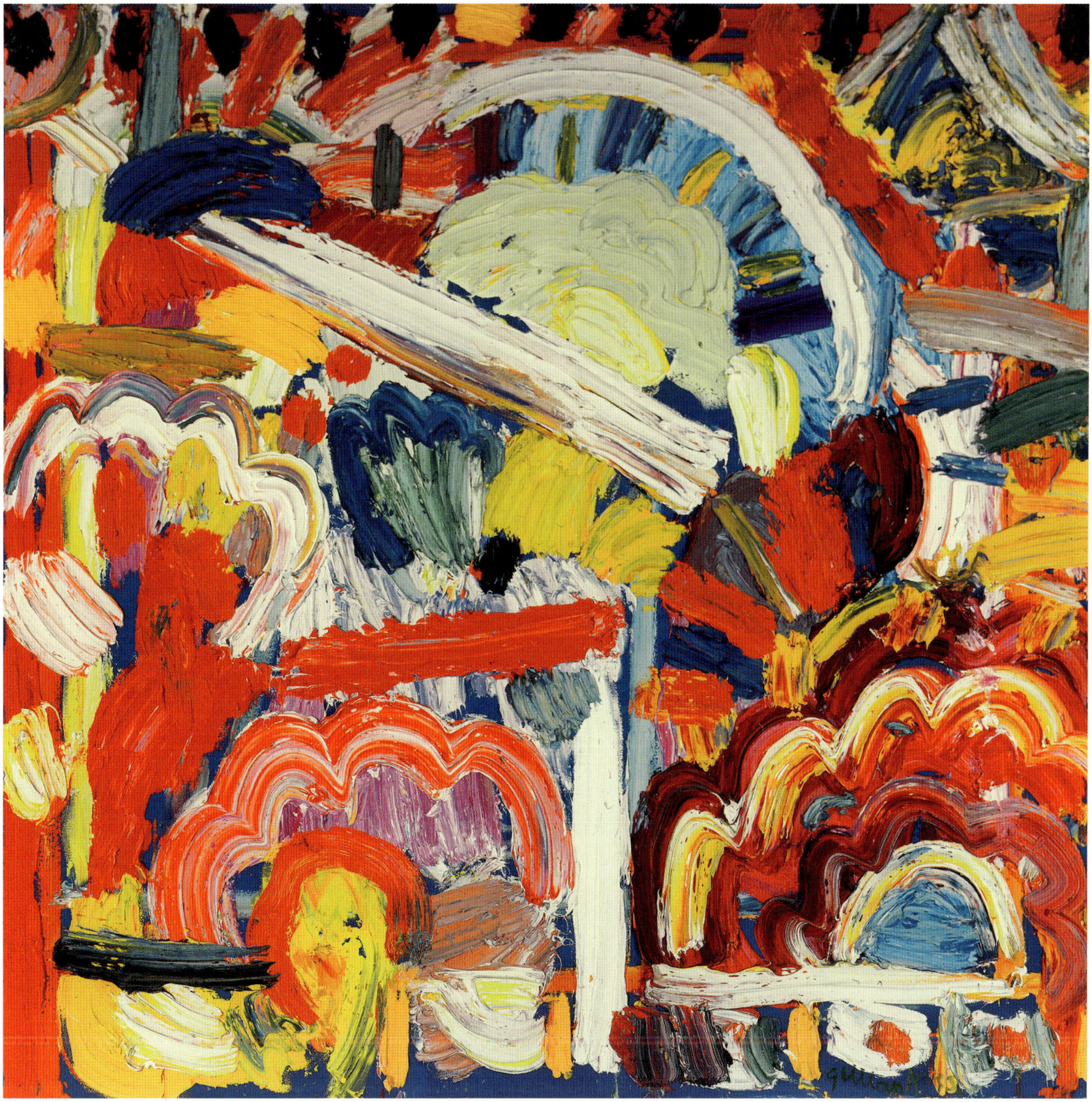

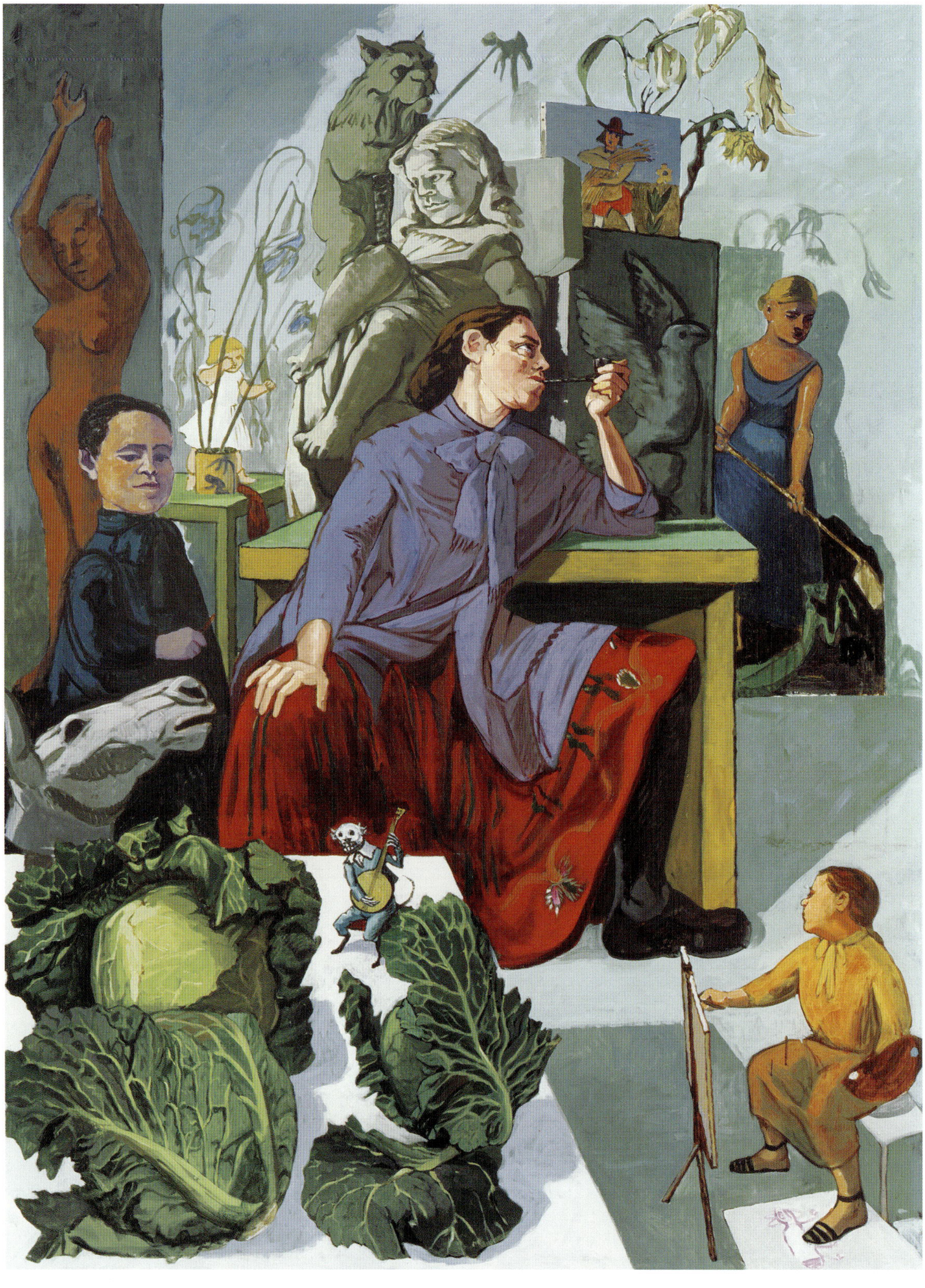

The Artist in Her Studio 1993

Paula Rego (born 1935)

Acrylic on canvas 180 x 130cm
Bought with the aid of grants from The Art Fund
and the Leeds Art Collections Fund 1994

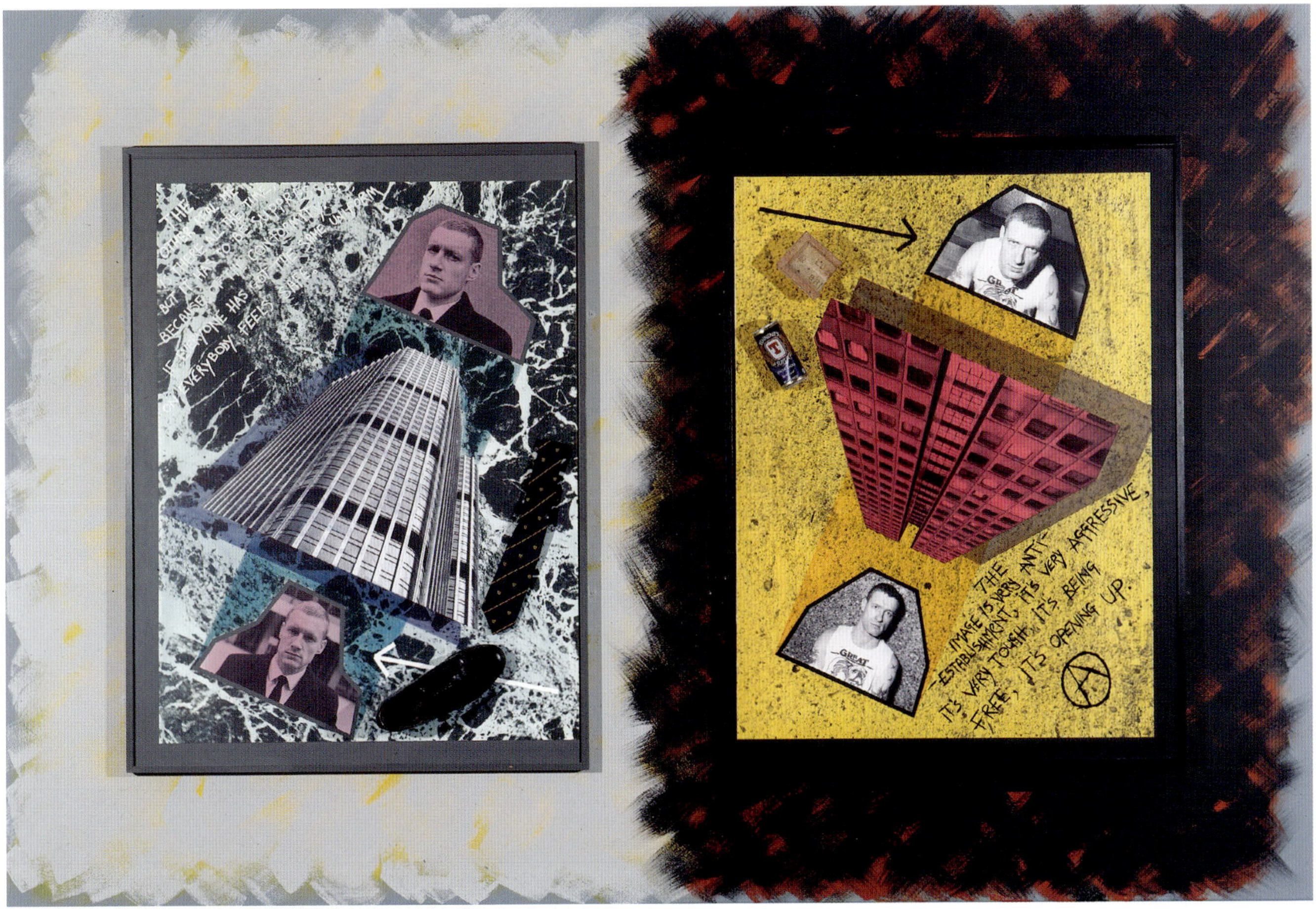

Doppelgänger 1984

Stephen Willats (born 1943)

Mixed media 136 x 98cm and 136 x 98cm
Bought 1989

Whisper the Wind the Waves 1993

Susan Lacy (born 1945)

Iwo text panels, eight photographs and video recording of performance in California, 1984
Bought from the artist with the aid of a grant from the V&A Purchase Grant Fund 1994

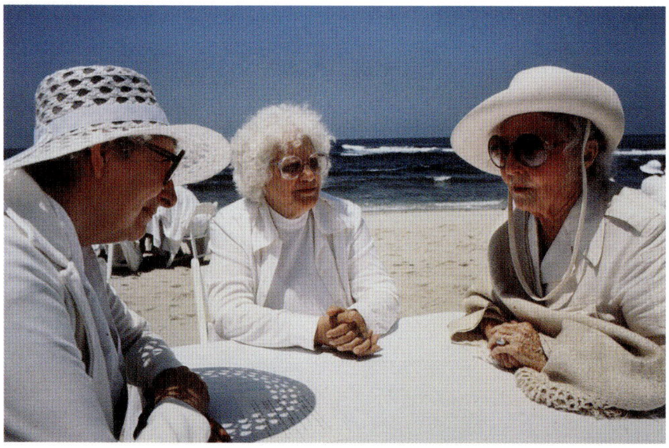

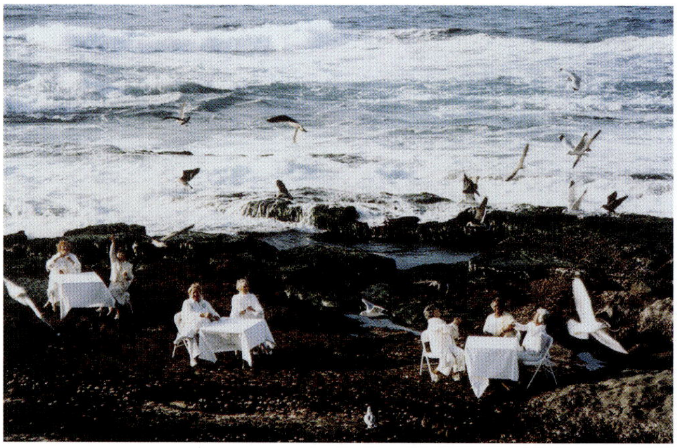

Erasers 1985

Tim Head (born 1946)

Cibachrome photograph 122 x 244cm
Bought from A Reynolds Gallery, with the aid of a grant from the Centre for the Study of Sculpture 1986

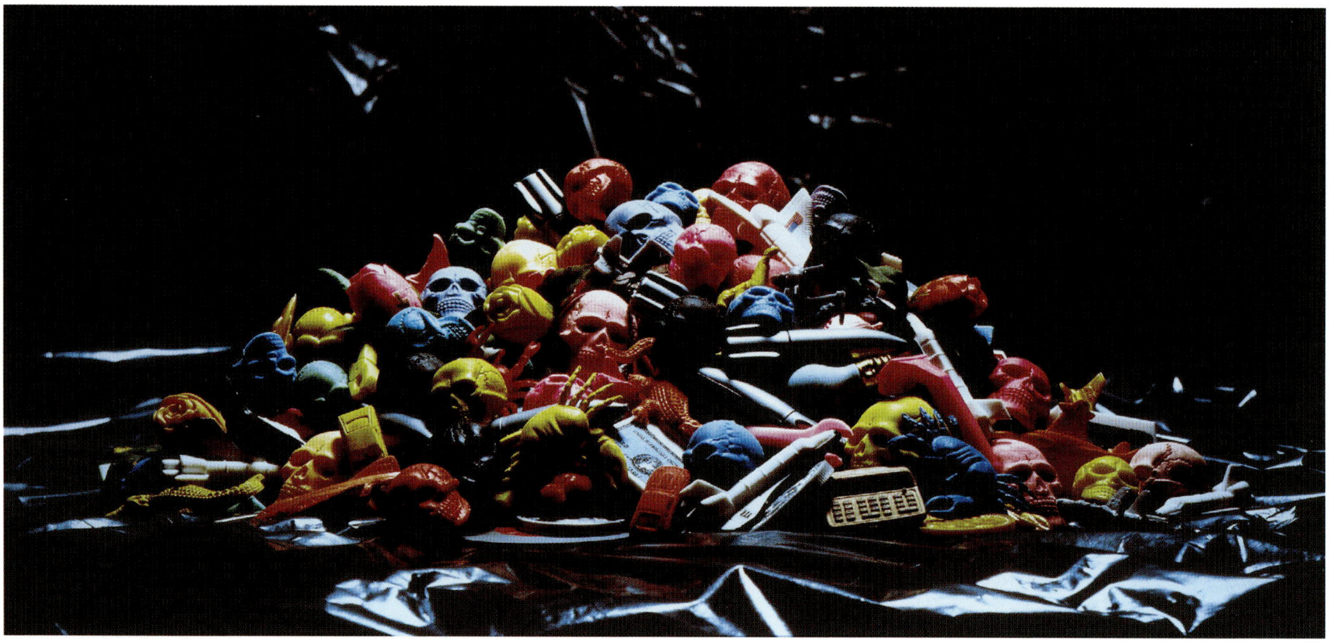

Big V 2004

Georgina Starr (born 1968)

Four-screen projection
Bought by the Contemporary Art Society on behalf of Leeds Art Gallery as part of the Special Collection Scheme funded by the Arts Council Lottery 2004

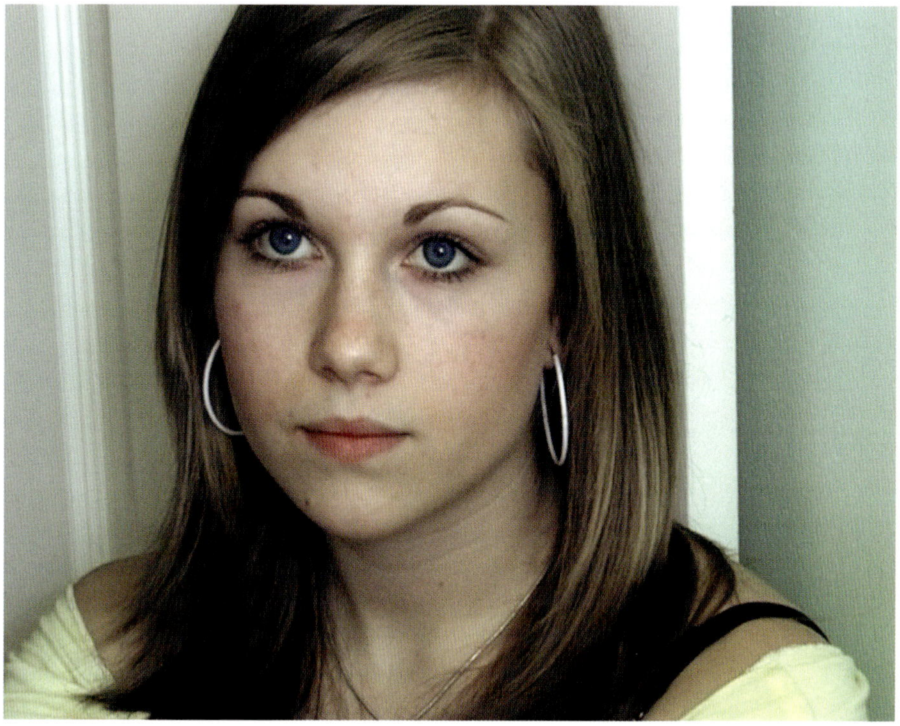

What Things Say About Us 2002

Grayson Perry (born 1960)

Glazed earthenware 57cm
Bought Laurent Delaye Gallery 2002

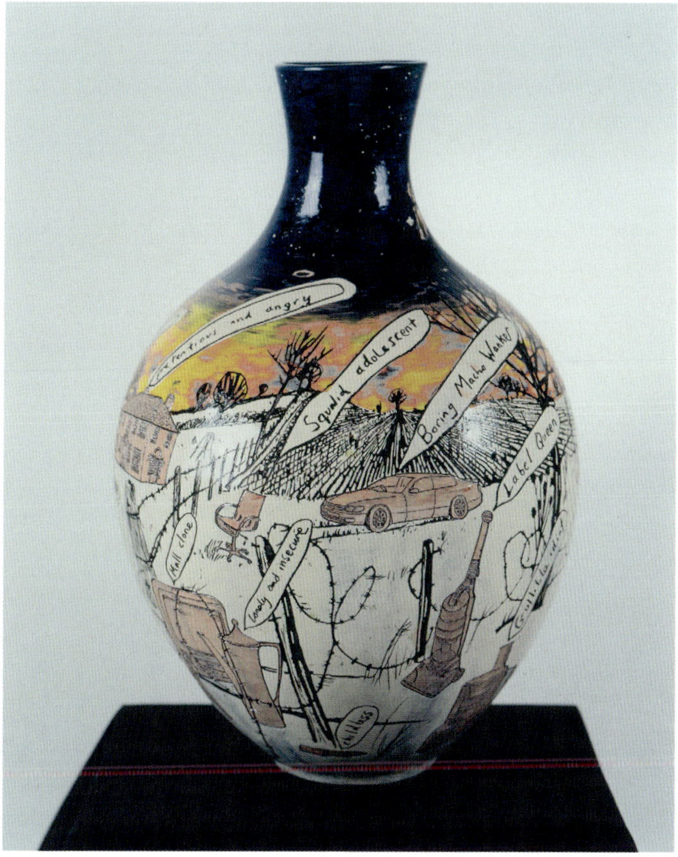

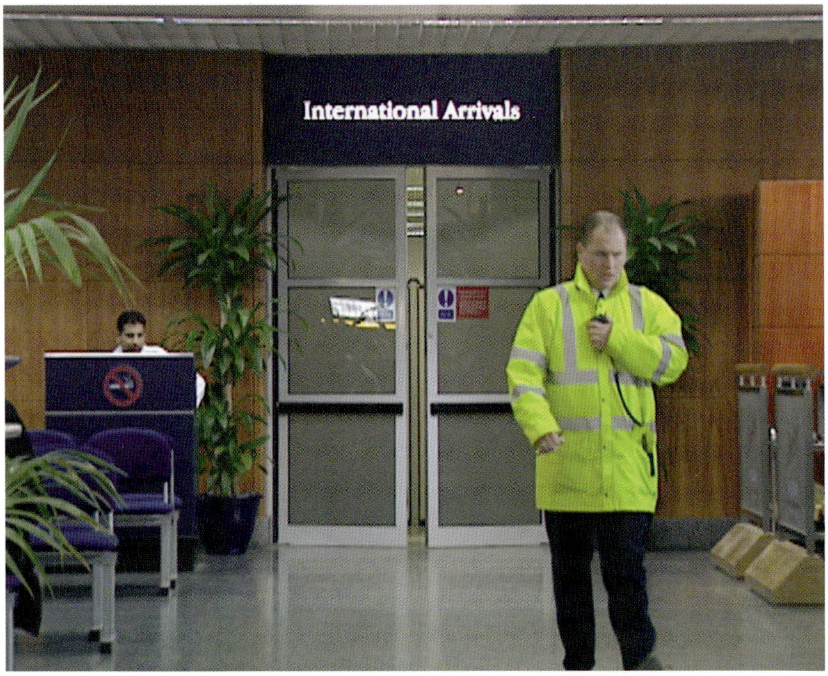

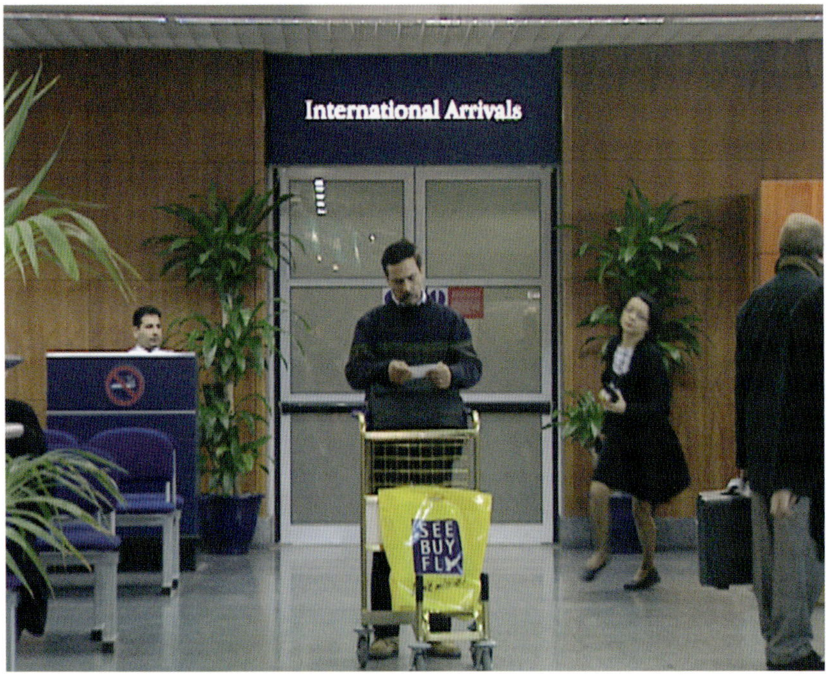

Threshold to the Kingdom 2000
Mark Wallinger (born 1959)
DitiBeta tape
Bought by the Contemporary Art Society on behalf of Leeds Art Gallery as part of the Special Collection Scheme funded by the Arts Council Lottery 2000

Primal Soundings 2004

Bill Fontana (born 1947)

Sound sculpture on DVD and CD
Bought by the Contemporary Art Society on behalf of Leeds Art Gallery as part of the Special Collection Scheme funded by the Arts Council Lottery 2004

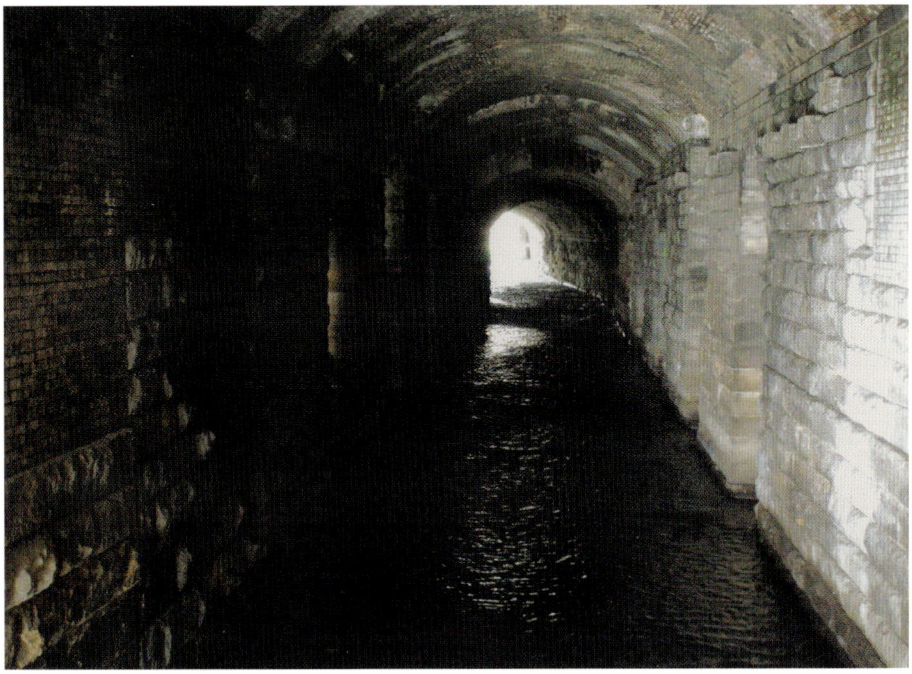

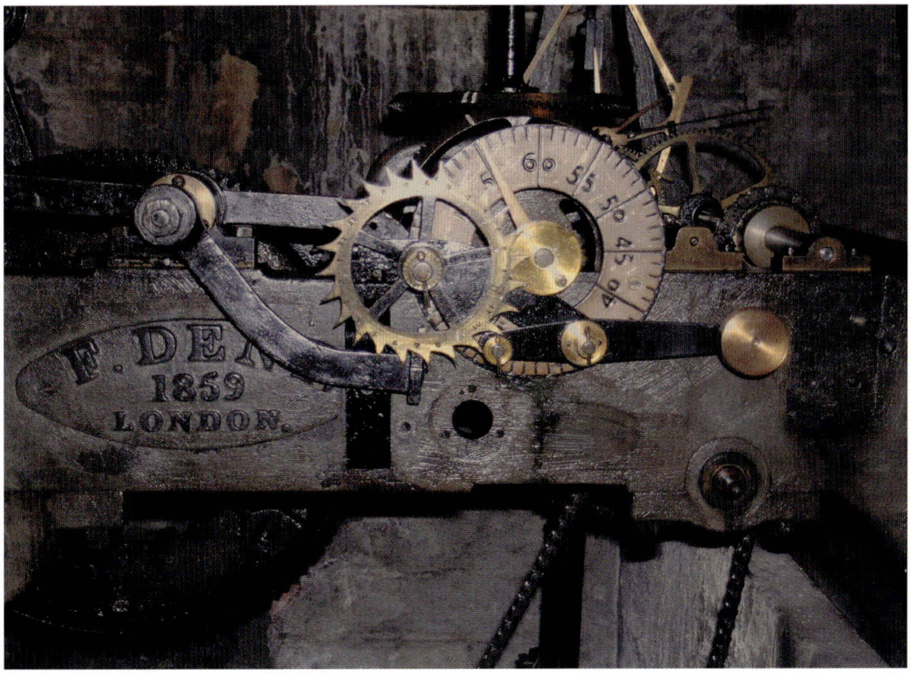

Works on Paper

In 1925 Robert Hawthorn Kitson, an amateur watercolour artist and a member of the Art Gallery sub-committee, set out to create *'a first rate general collection of watercolours, a thing that doesn't exist in England, the home of watercolour painting, it is a big ambition...'*

In the inter-war years the acquisition of watercolours became the main focus of collecting, with a number of major purchases including *The Ploughed Field* by John Sell Cotman and *Lake Albano and Castel Gandulfo* by John Robert Cozens. Collectors were actively courted leading to notable bequests. On his death in 1937 the majority of the collection of drawings and watercolours such as *Barnard Castle from Towler Hill* by John Sell Cotman, which had been amassed by Robert's uncle, Sydney Kitson, was deposited at the Gallery. Sydney Kitson, a Leeds architect, called his obsession 'Cotmania', and the material formed the basis of his definitive biography of the artist. In 1952 brother and sister, Agnes and Norman Lupton, bequeathed one of the finest collections of English watercolours in private hands.

The Lupton bequest included not only major works by leading English watercolourists of the late 18TH and 19TH centuries, but also a sequence from Turner's prints for the *Liber Studiorum* and 64 etchings by Rembrandt.

With the appointment of Philip Hendy as Director in 1934 the pattern of collecting shifted back to painting and sculpture. Nonetheless, in recent years, there have been notable additions to the works on paper collection. In 1991 the Professor Robert Holmes bequest strengthened the holding of Neo-Romantic works and added the first original work by David Hockney, a pen and ink drawing, *Peter Reading at Anguillara*. The Gallery continues to build the collection to represent work by living artists. The Contemporary Art Society presented 'Glasgow Boy' Ken Currie's gritty, tour de force *In the City Bar*, which explodes the notion of drawing as intimate in scale. Historic works, with strong Yorkshire connections, such as *The Valley of the Washburn* by JMW Turner, a watercolour originally owned by Walter Fawkes of Farnley Hall, have been acquired with the help of Lottery funding.

Today Leeds can boast one of the finest collections of works on paper in Britain, with around 10,000 items which date from about 1450 to the present day. There are regularly changing displays from the collection in the Gallery but, due to the fragility of the medium, display time has to be limited, and the majority of the works are housed in the Print Room where they can be viewed by appointment.

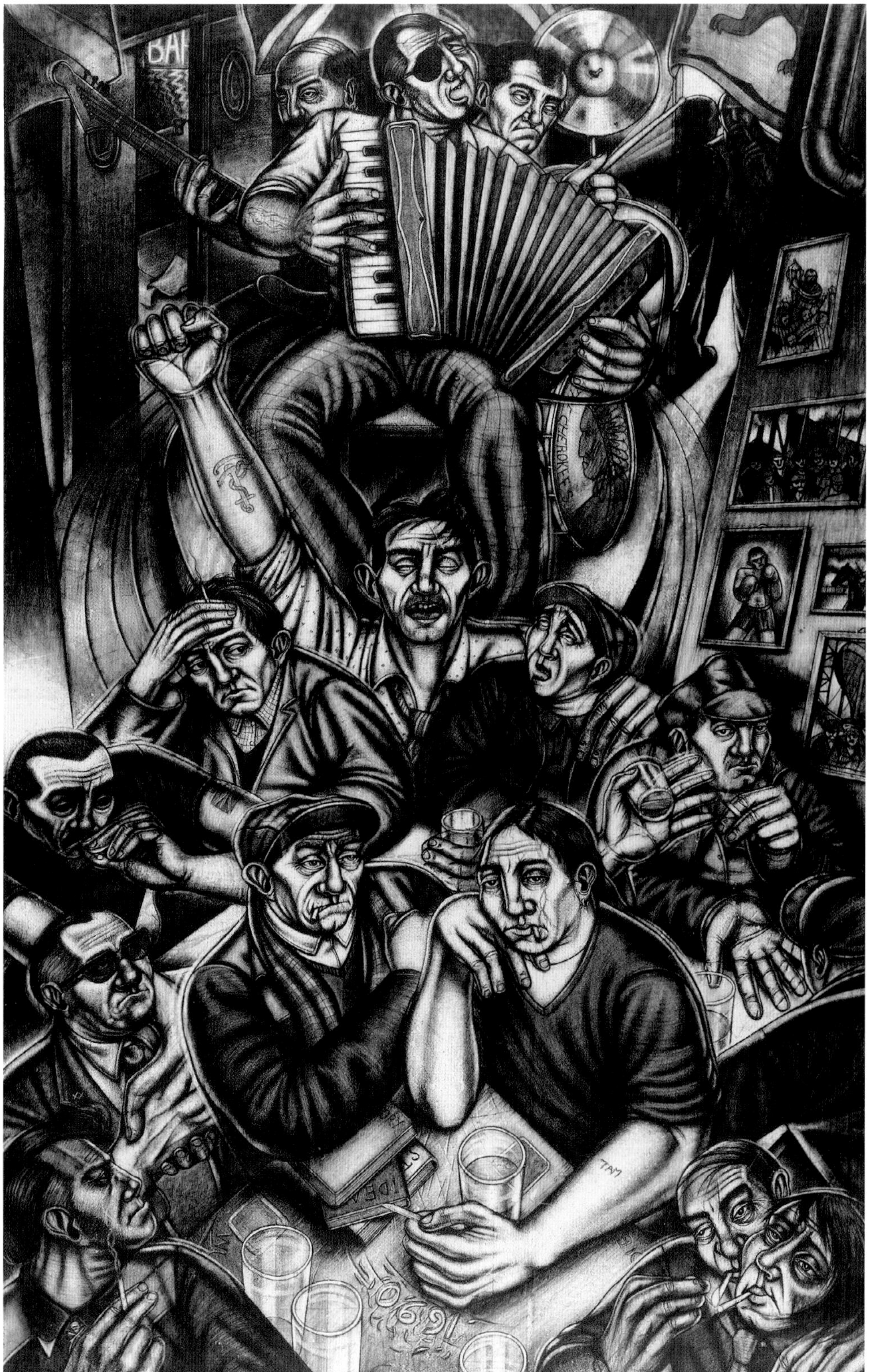

In the City Bar... Disillusion 1985

Ken Currie (born 1960)

Conté crayon on wove paper 238.7 x 152.4cm
Presented by the Contemporary Art Society 1988

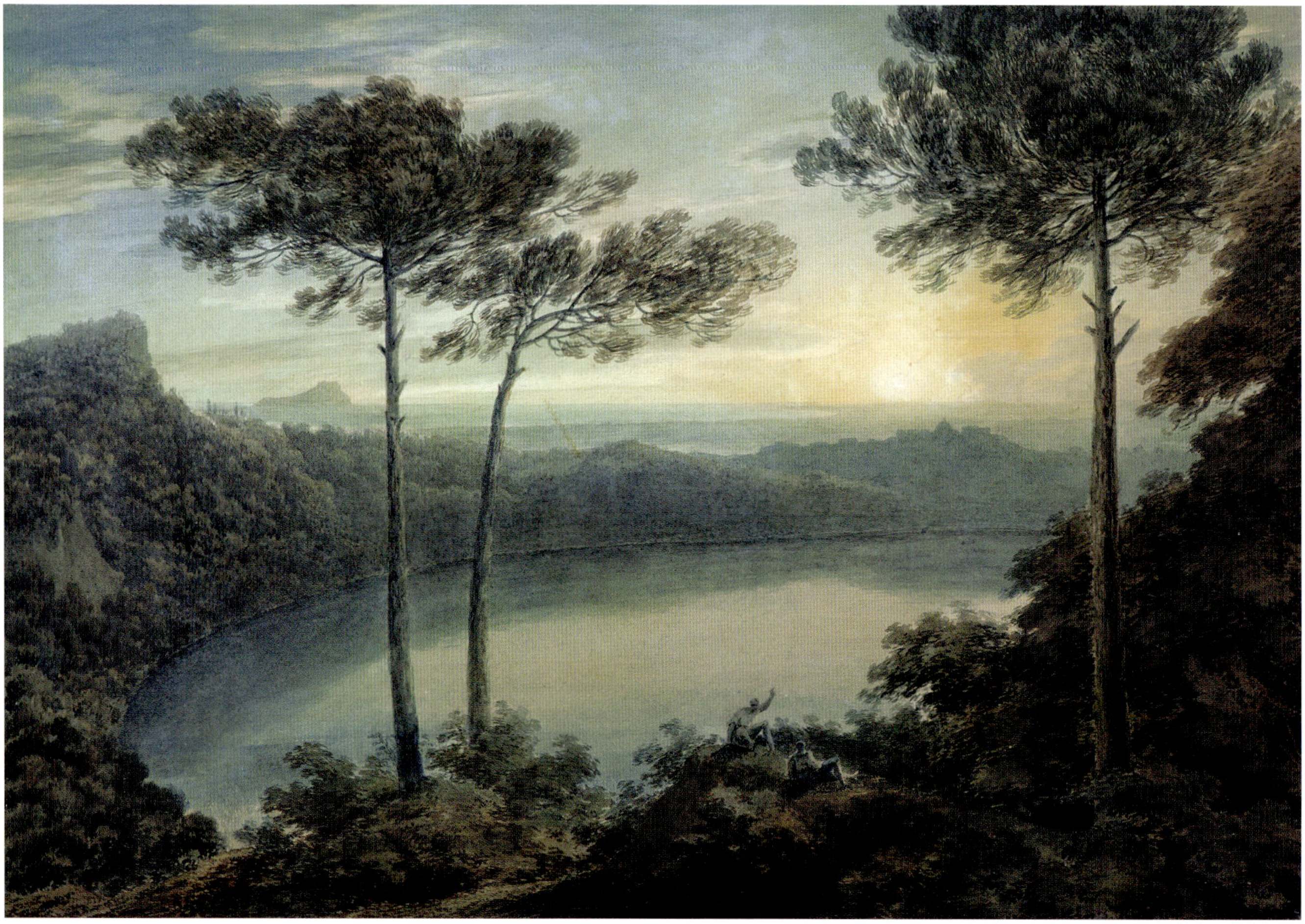

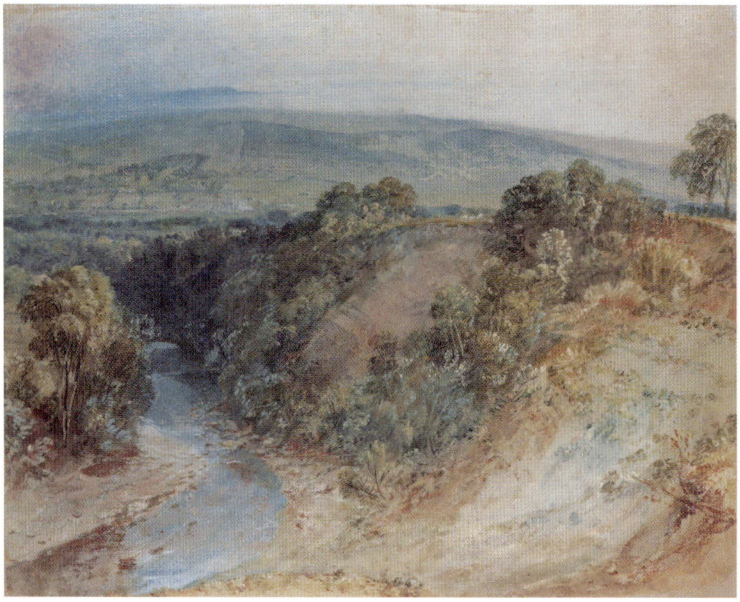

ABOVE

Lake Albano and Castel Gandolfo

John Robert Cozens (1752–1797)

Watercolour on laid paper 60.2 x 85.4cm
Given by Herbert M Hepworth, Robert H Kitson and Agnes and Norman Lupton 1928

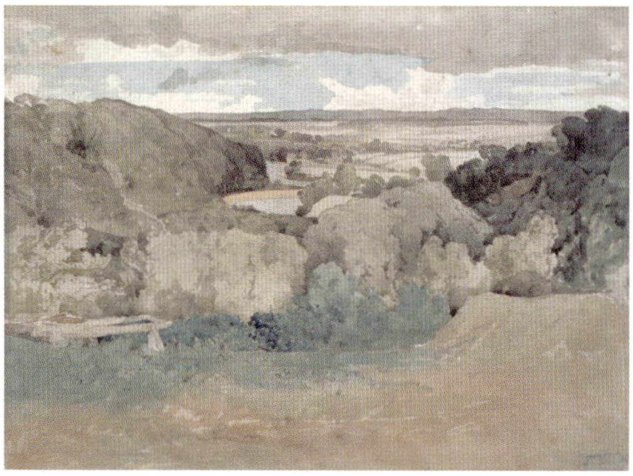

OPPOSITE BOTTOM LEFT

The Valley of the Washburn c1818

Joseph Mallord William Turner (1775–1851)

Watercolour over pencil on wove paper 172.5 x 215.9cm
Bought with the aid of grants from the Heritage Lottery Fund, The Art Fund and the Leeds Art Collections Fund 1997

OPPOSITE BOTTOM RIGHT

Barnard Castle from Towler Hill c1806

John Sell Cotman (1782–1842)

Watercolour over pencil on laid paper 33.1 x 43.7cm
Sydney Decimus Kitson bequest 1937

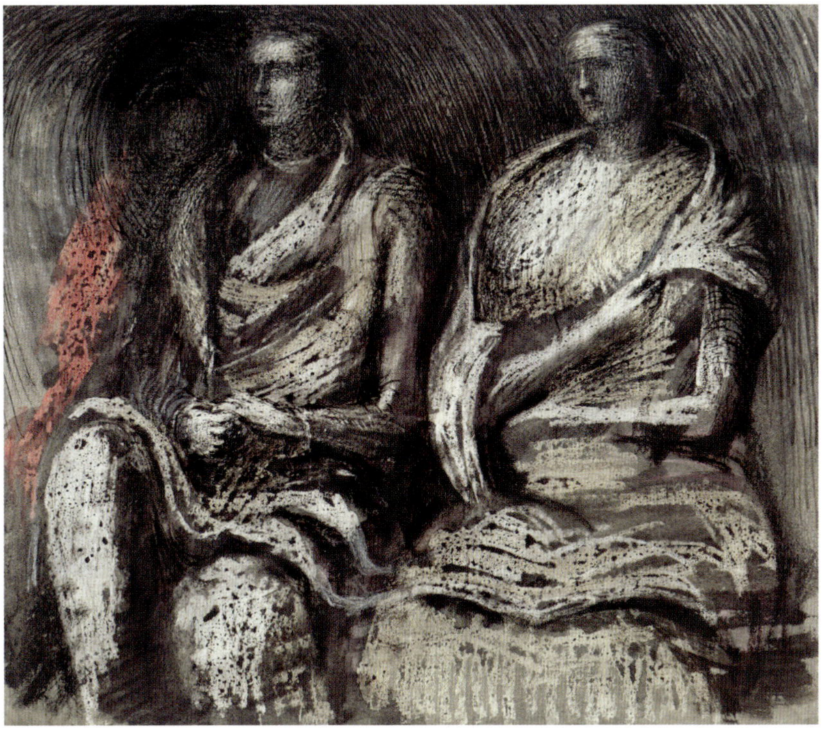

Shelter Scene – Two Seated Figures 1941

Henry Moore (1898–1986)

Watercolour, crayon and ink on paper 38 x 42.8cm
Presented by the War Artists Advisory Committee 1947

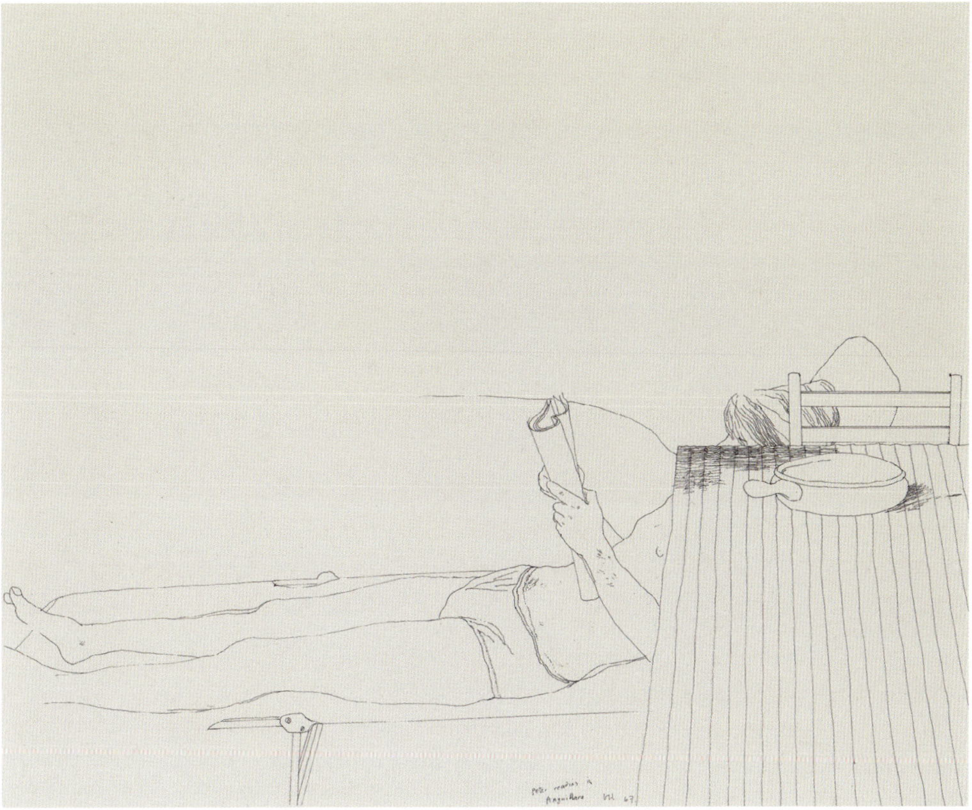

Peter Reading in Anguillara 1967

David Hockney (born 1937)

Pen and ink on wove paper 38 x 42.8cm
Professor Robert Holmes bequest 1991

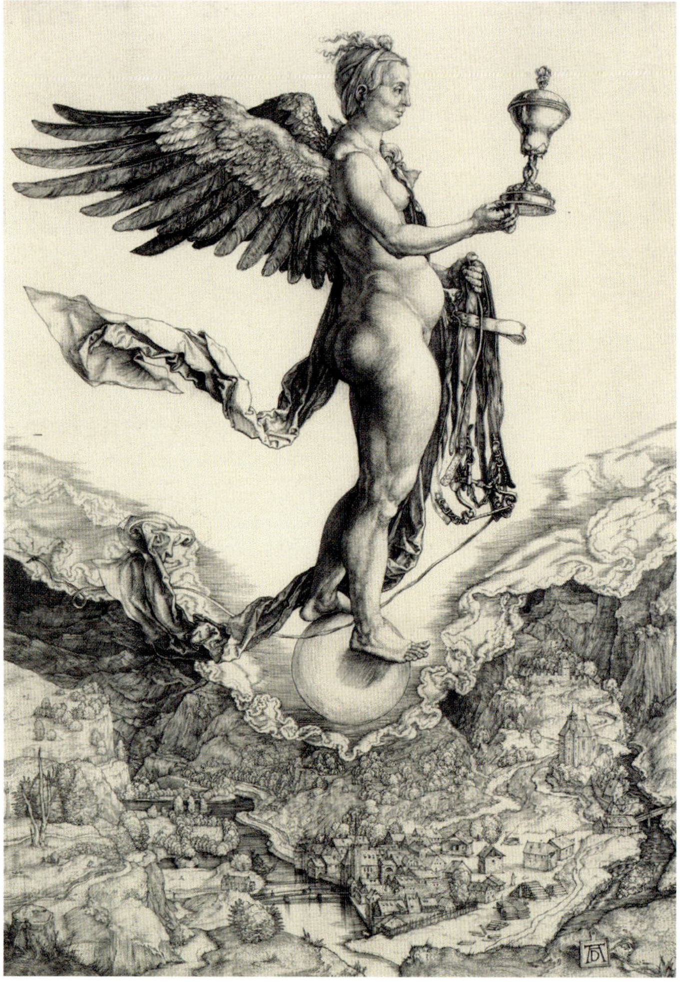

Nemesis (The Great Fortune) c1501–02
Albrecht Dürer (1471–1528)
Engraving 33.3 x 22.9cm
Agnes and Norman Lupton bequest 1952

York Road, Leeds
Sir Muirhead Bone (1876–1953)
Etching 20 x 27.8cm
Bought 1908

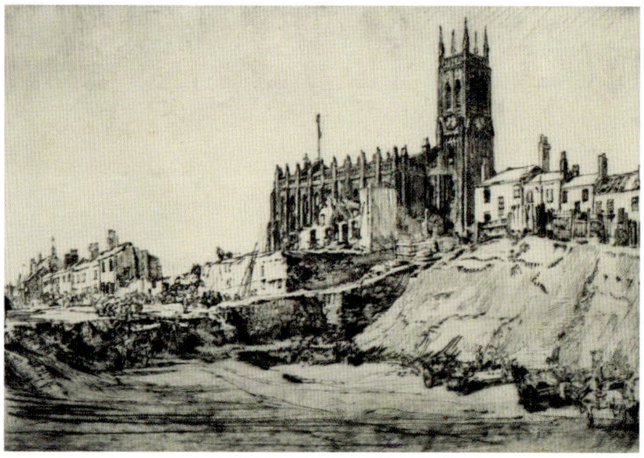

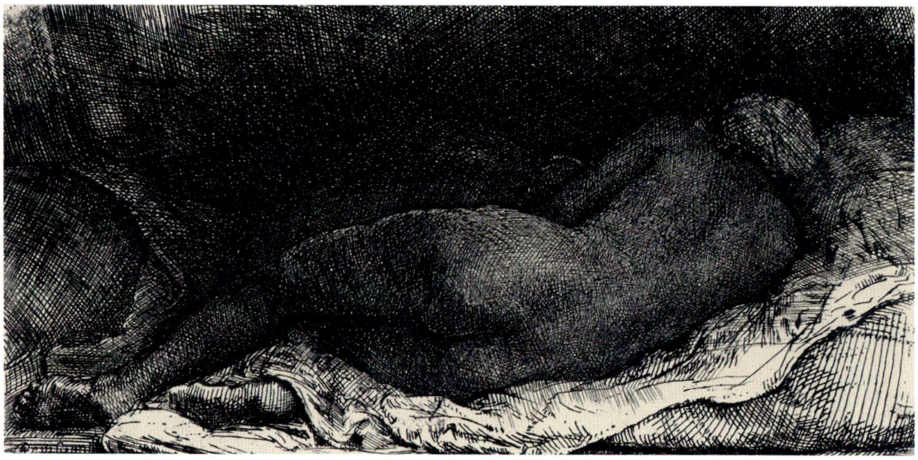

The Negress Lying Down 1658
Rembrandt van Rijn (1606–1669)
Etching and drypoint 8.2 x 15.8cm
Agnes and Norman Lupton bequest 1952

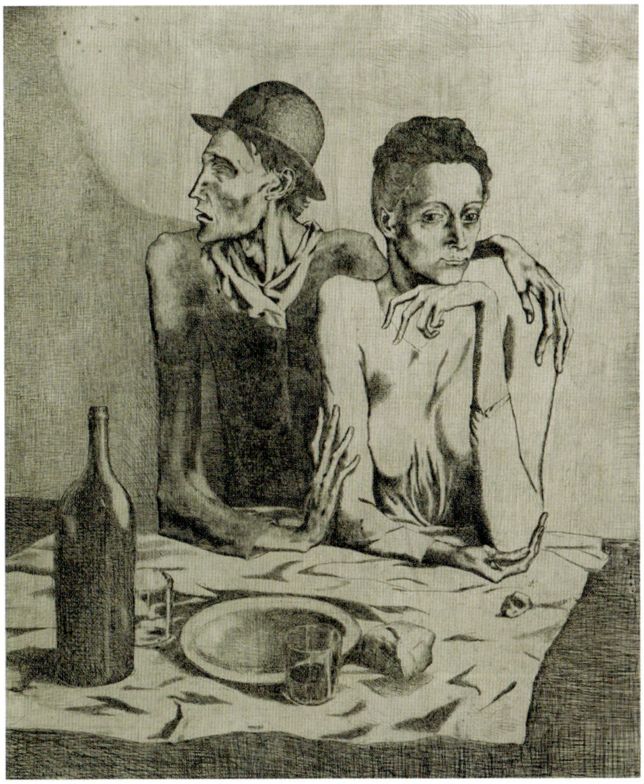

Le Repas Frugal (The Frugal Meal) 1913

Pablo Picasso (1881–1973)

Engraving 46.3 x 37.9cm
Presented by Mrs F Gott 1937

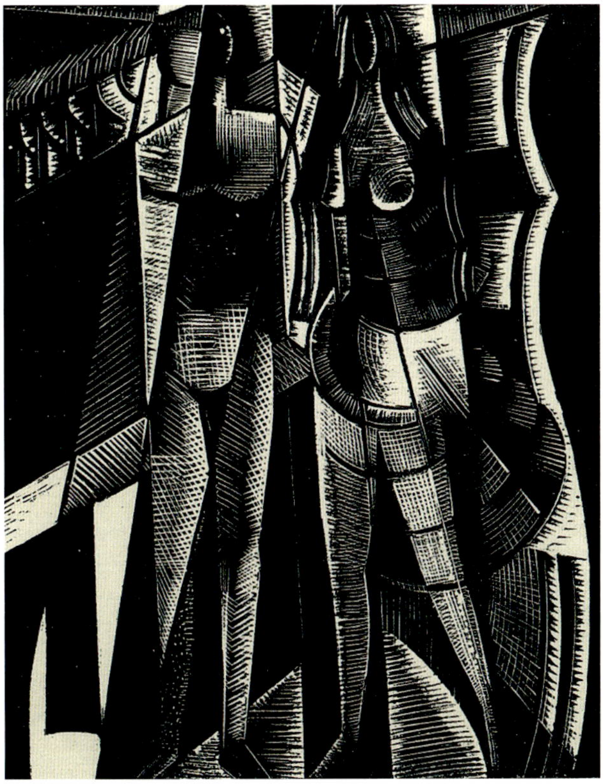

The Book of Genesis 1924

Paul Nash (1889–1946)

Book with 12 woodcut illustrations, edition 255/350, 27.7 x 19.7cm
Bought by the Leeds Art Collections Fund from Gallery 39 1979

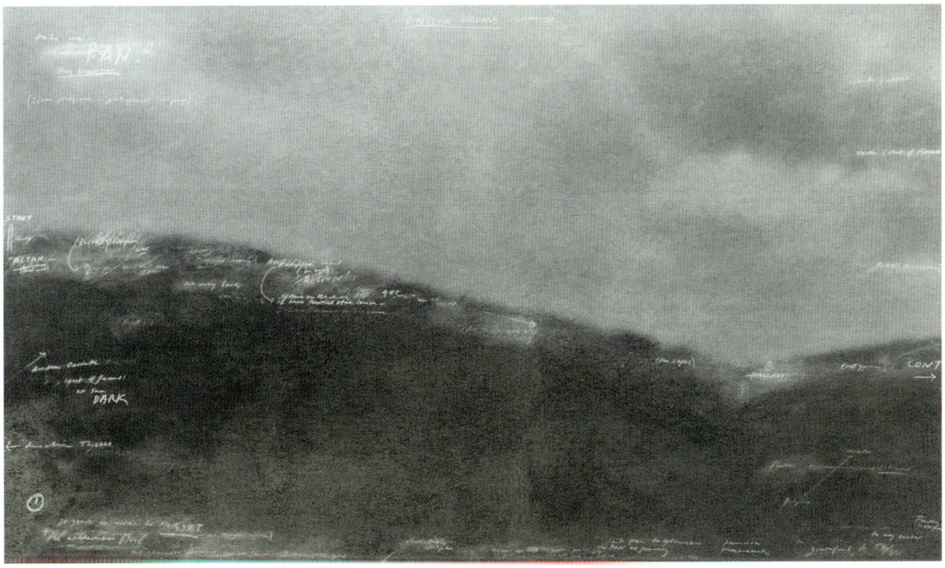

Blind Pan 2004

Tacita Dean (born 1965)

Series of five photogravures on Hahnemule paper, edition 11/24
Bought from Frith Street Gallery 2005

Sculpture at Leeds

Leeds Art Gallery is rich in British sculpture dating from the late 19TH century onwards, though it also has works from earlier centuries and other parts of Europe.

Successive Directors of the Art Gallery, such as Philip Hendy (1934–1945) and Robert Rowe (1958–1983) established a reputation for the perceptive collecting of early modern and contemporary sculpture, acquiring works by Jacob Epstein, Henri Gaudier-Brzeska, Barbara Hepworth and Henry Moore. The Gregory Fellowship in sculpture at Leeds University, founded in the 1950s, brought new young artists, such as Hubert Dalwood, Neville Boden and Bill Tucker to the city and sales of their pieces to the Gallery. In addition, the collection has benefited greatly from donations by the Leeds Art Collections Fund, and national funding bodies. However, it was the introduction of support from the Henry Moore Foundation, beginning in 1982, and its establishment of the Henry Moore Institute in 1993, which really confirmed Leeds as an international centre for the study and appreciation of sculpture.

The collection, which includes maquettes, models and works on paper, as well as finished sculptures, has doubled in size since then. It seeks to represent the broad spectrum of British sculptural practice in the 20TH century, from the monumental and architectural to the more private and personal, and from the 'Academic' to the avant-garde. It places artists such as William Hamo Thornycroft, AH Gerrard, Peter Peri, Bernard Schottlander and Betty Rea, whose contributions are often omitted from conventional histories of modern British sculpture, alongside others such as Epstein, Hepworth and Moore, whose names are still well-known.

More recent acquisitions are by Eric Gill, Frank Dobson, Michael Kenny, Stuart Brisley, Alison Wilding and Eva Rothschild. In conjunction with the sculpture collection, the Henry Moore Institute has developed the Gallery's rich archive of papers relating to British sculptors (many of whom are represented in the collection), including personal papers, correspondence, diaries, casting ledgers, photographs and sketch books.

The archive is open by appointment in the Institute building next door to the Art Gallery.

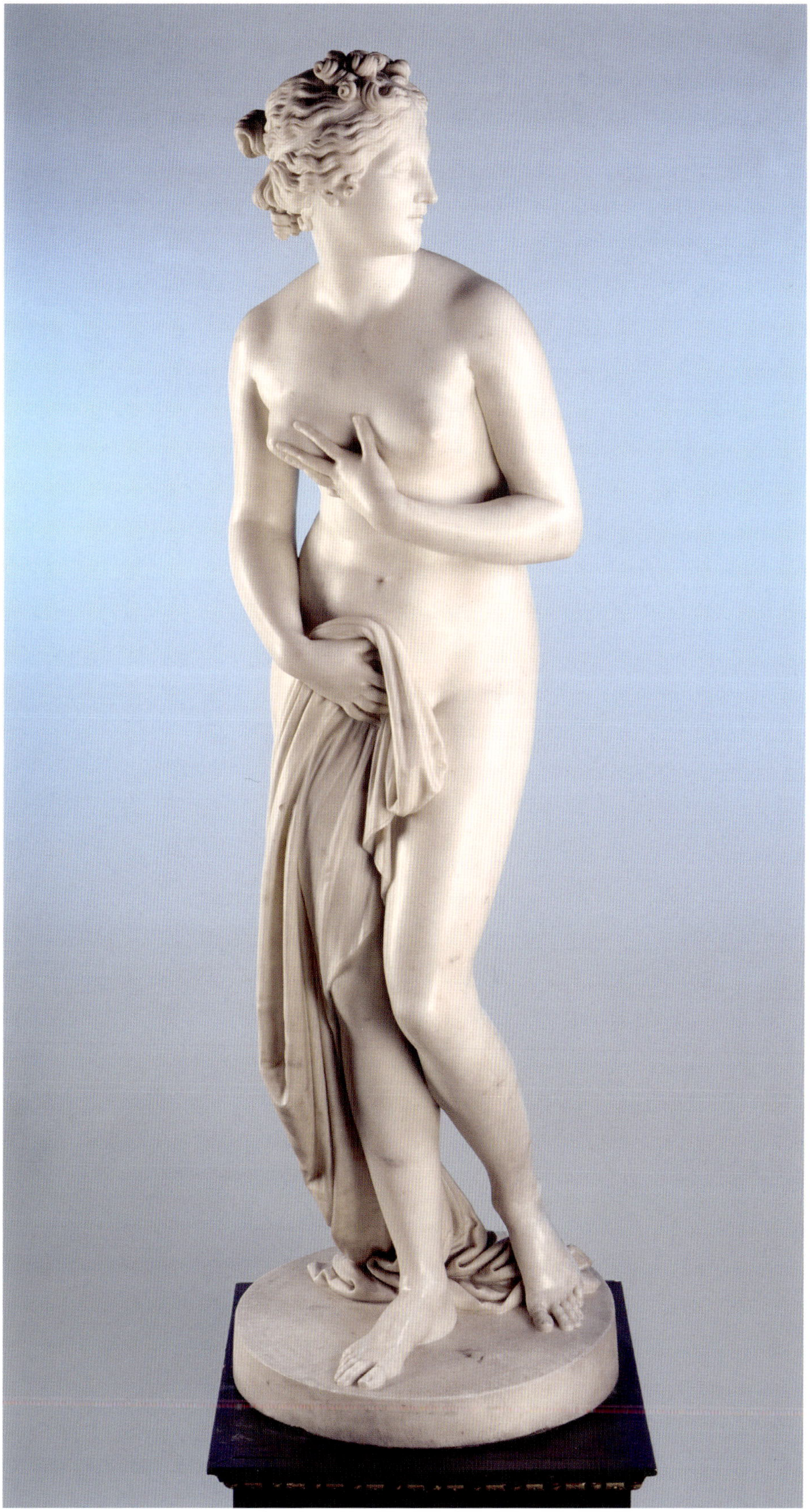

Venus 1817–20

Antonio Canova (1757–1822)

Marble 177 x 52 x 70cm
Presented by Mrs Dorothy Una McGrigor-Phillips 1959

This statue is based on a Roman original in the Uffizi Gallery, Florence, and is the last of four produced by Canova to a similar design. The sculptor is said to have been more satisfied with this version than any of those made earlier

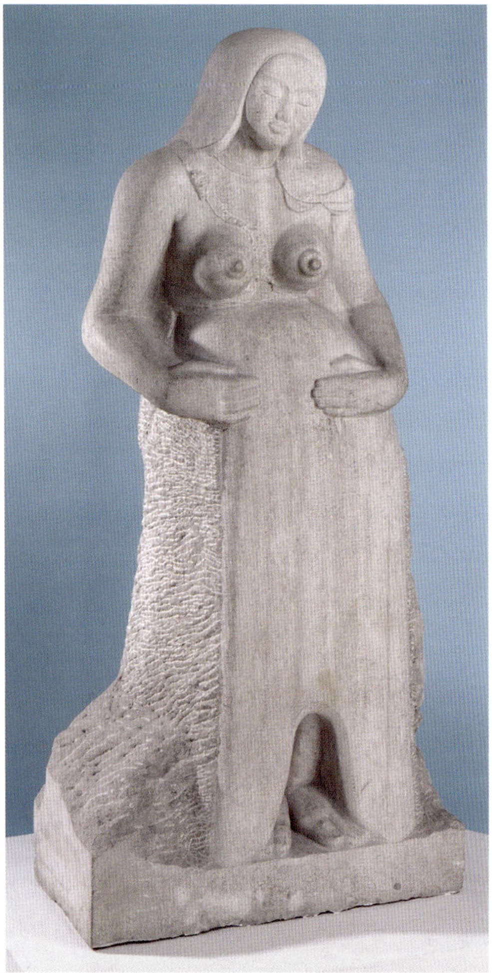

Maternity 1910

Jacob Epstein (1880–1959)

Hopton Wood stone 203 x 91 x 46cm
Bought with the aid of grants from The Art Fund, the National Heritage Memorial Fund and various private benefactors 1983

Maternity was first exhibited at the Royal Albert Hall in 1912, where it received a hostile reaction from critics. It may have been intended as part of a *'great scheme of doing some colossal figures... a sort of twentieth century Stone Henge'*, which Epstein planned with the sculptor, Eric Gill in 1910, though the project was never realized

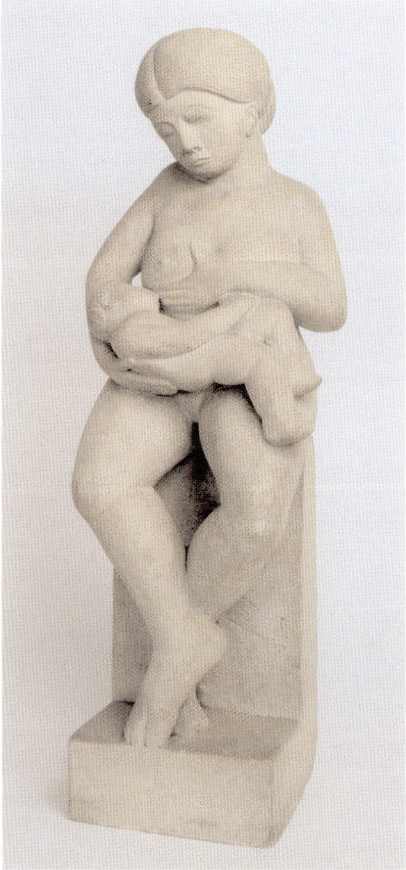

Mother and Child 1910

Eric Gill (1882–1940)

Portland stone 62.2 x 20.3 x 17.1cm
Bought with the aid of grants from the National Heritage Memorial Fund, the V&A Purchase Grant Fund and the Pilgrim Trust 1995

This is one of a trio of 'Mother and Child' carvings which were the first fully three-dimensional pieces carved by Gill, who originally trained as a lettercutter

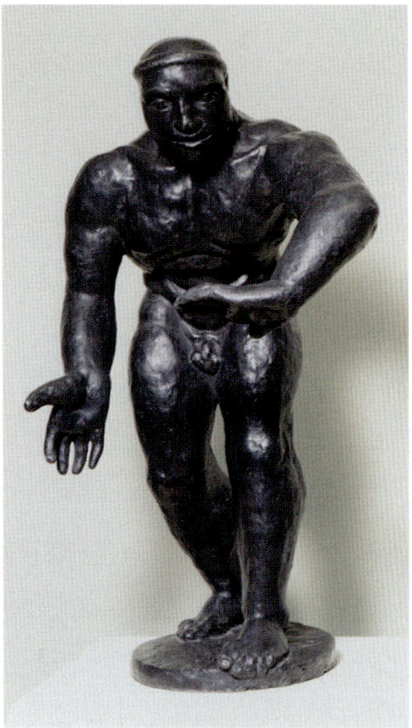

The Wrestler 1912

Henri Gaudier-Brzeska (1891–1915)

Lead 64.5 x 29.4 x 37.5cm
Bought with the aid of a grant from the Board of Education 1943

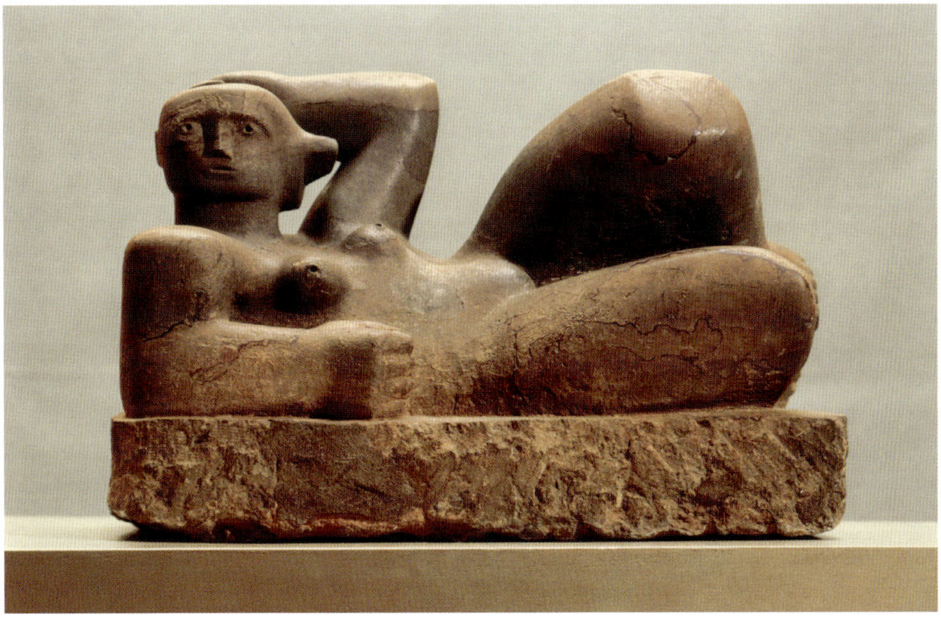

Reclining Figure 1929
Henry Moore (1898–1986)
Hornton stone 54 x 82 x 37cm
Bought with the aid of a grant from the Board of Education 1941

This is among the first of Moore's 'Reclining Figures', a theme which was to preoccupy his work for the rest of his life

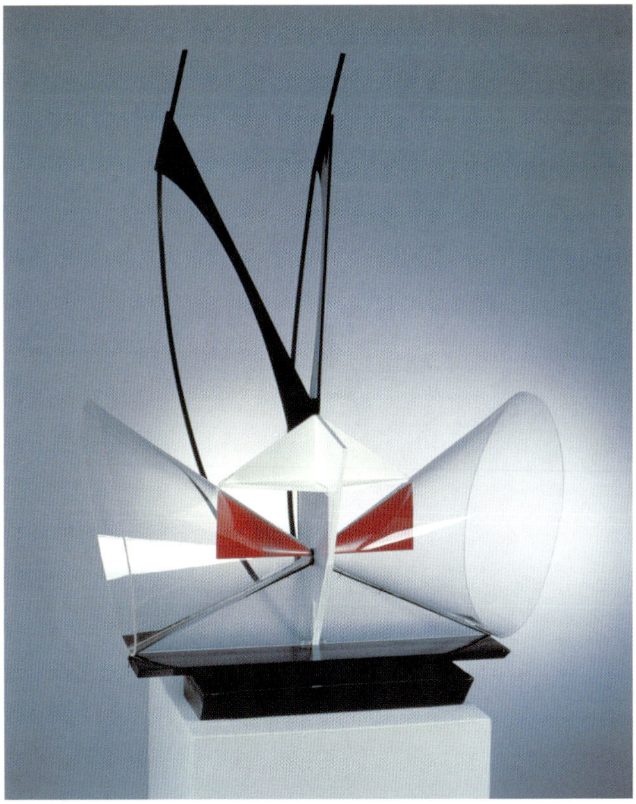

Construction in Space: Soaring 1930
Naum Gabo (1880–1977)
Brass, plexiglass and wood 112 x 77 x 71cm
Accepted by HM Government in lieu of inheritance tax and allocated to Leeds Museums & Galleries 1989

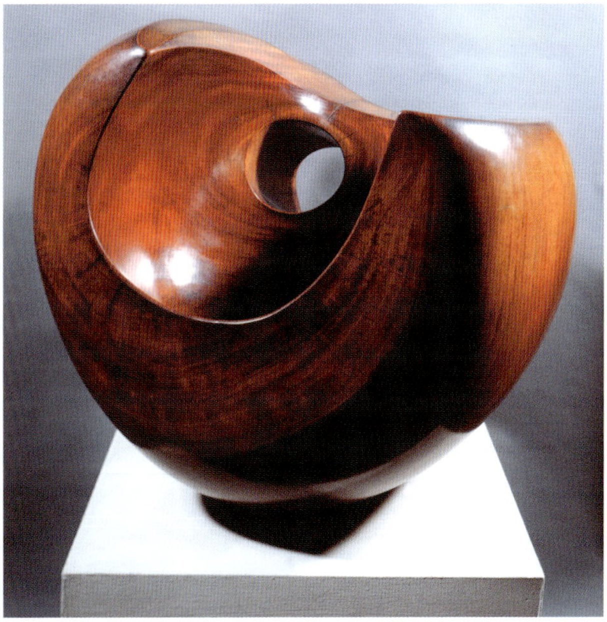

Configuration (Phira) 1955
Barbara Hepworth (1903–1975)
Scented Guarea wood 68 x 68 x 64cm
Bought by the Leeds Art Collections Fund 1958

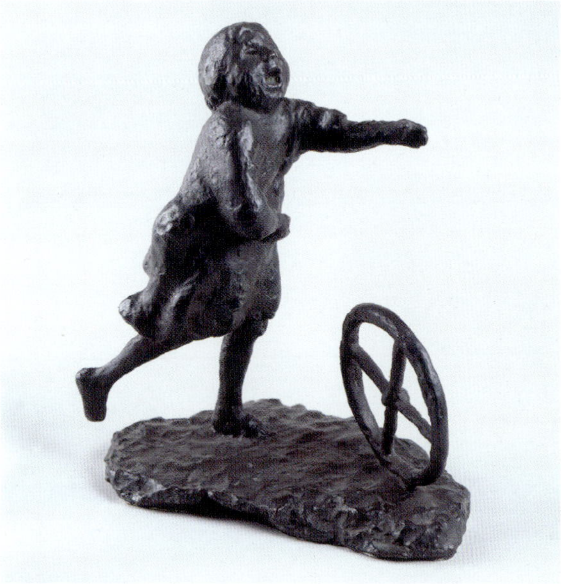

Running Girl with Wheel 1954

Ralph Brown (born 1928)

Bronze 25 x 30.5 x 15cm
Bought from the artist by the Leeds Art Collections Fund 1958

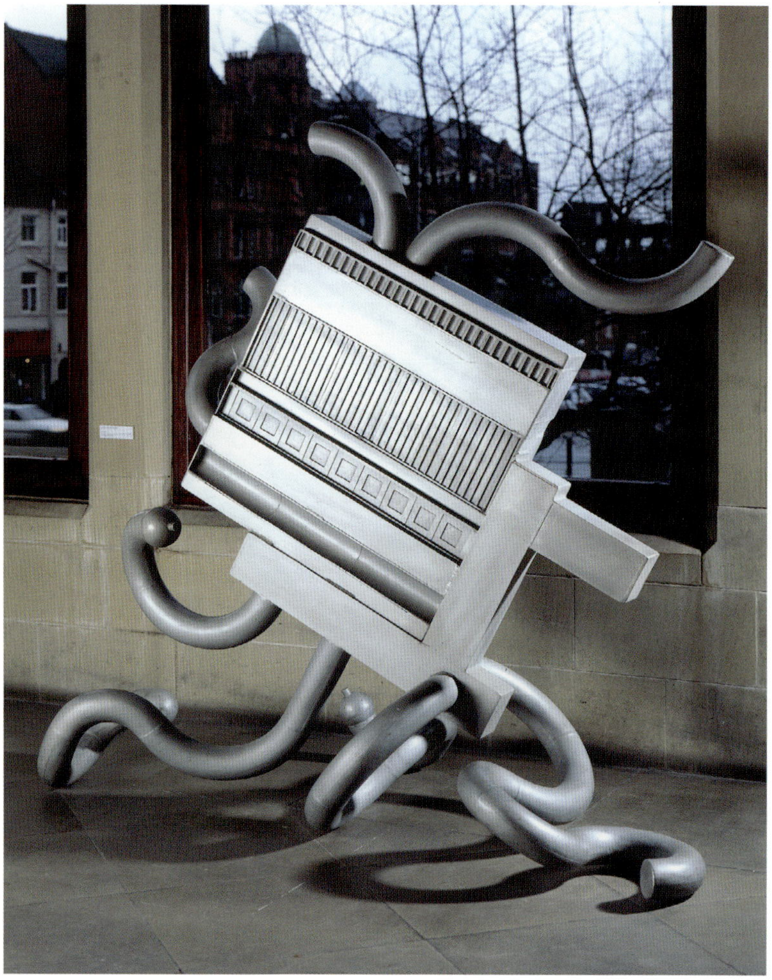

Poem for the Trio MRT 1964

Eduardo Paolozzi (1924–2005)

Aluminium 210 x 209 x 112cm
Bought with the aid of grants from the Gulbenkian Foundation, the V&A Purchase Grant Fund and the Leeds Art Collections Fund 1977

The letters MRT stand for Malevich, Rodchenko and Tatlin. *Poem for the Trio MRT* is intended to suggest an updated version of the classic marble sculpture of the *Laocoon* (showing a Trojan priest and his two sons being strangled by a serpent), as it might have been interpreted by these three Constructivist artists

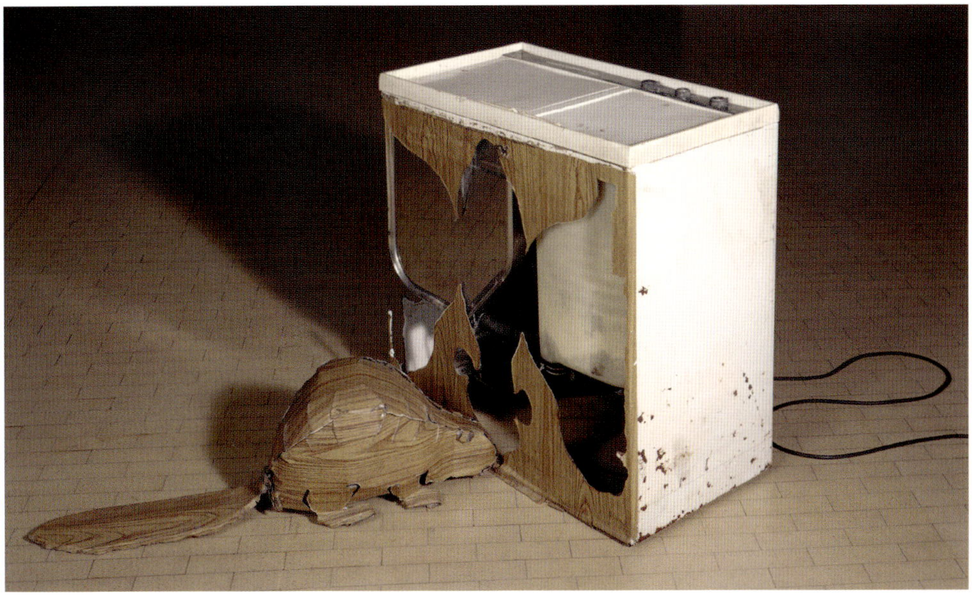

Twin-Tub with Beaver 1981

Bill Woodrow (born 1948)

Mixed media 78.5 × 73 × 41cm
Presented by the Contemporary Art Society 1986

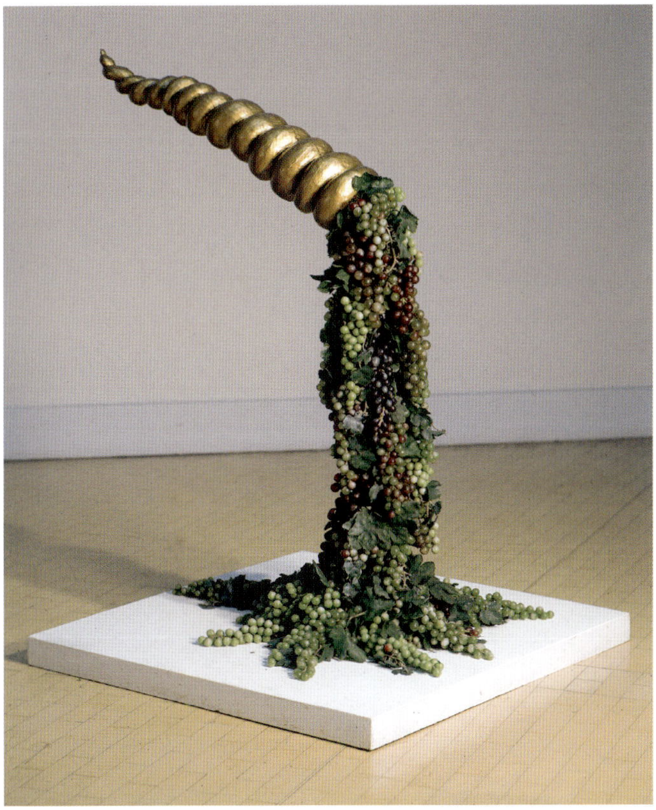

Fruit of Oblivion 1982

Edward Allington (born 1951)

Plastic grapes, unglazed ceramics, steel and metal 127 × 64 × 72cm
Bought from the artist with the aid of grants from the V&A Purchase Grant Fund and the Leeds Art Collections Fund 1995

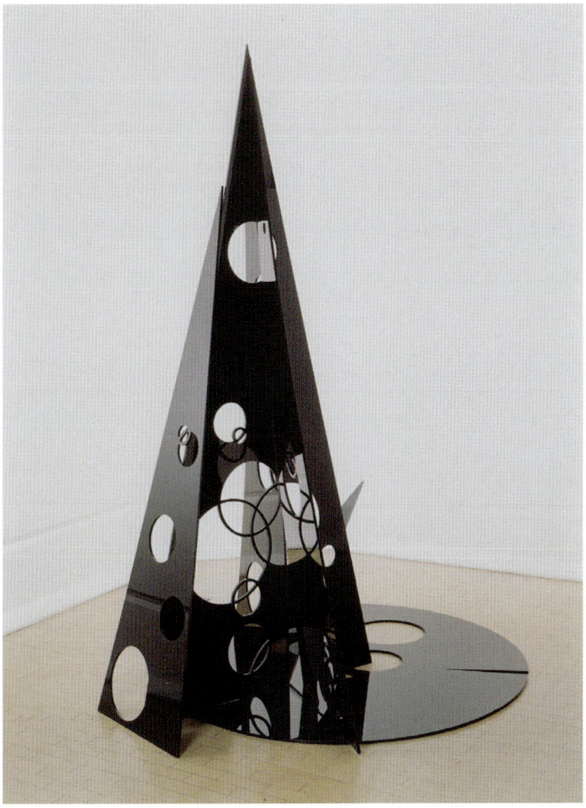

Bad Hat 2002

Eva Rothschild (born 1972)

Perspex 239 × 163 × 142cm
Bought with the aid of grants from the MLA/V&A Purchase Grant Fund and the Leeds Art Collections Fund 2002

Medicine Wheel 1982–83

Chris Drury (born 1948)

Mixed media 221.5cm
Presented by the artist (Victoria Miro Gallery)
and Coracle Press 1987

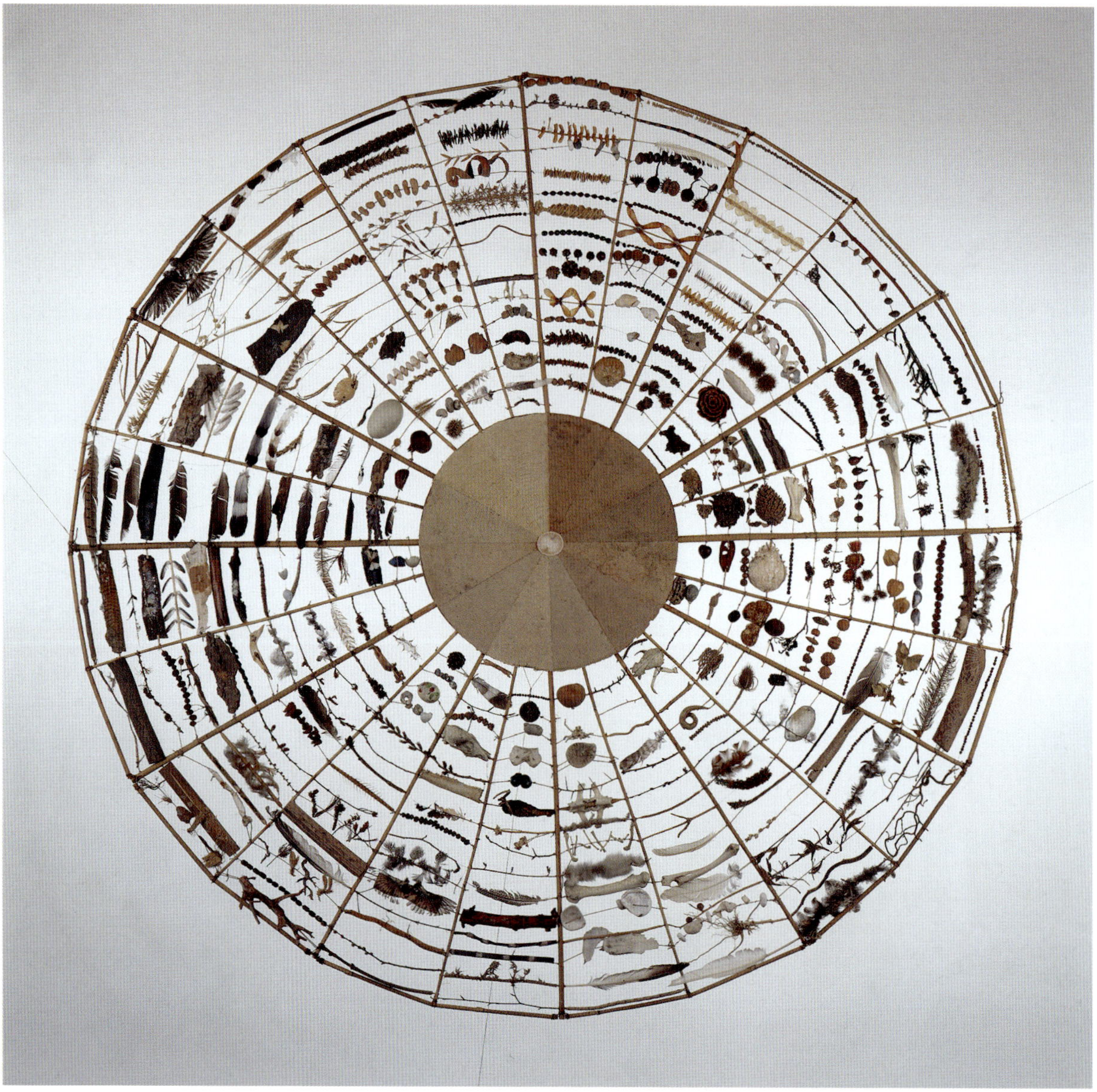

List of Artists

61 Edward Allington
40 Frank Auerbach
43 Gillian Ayres
37 Francis Bacon
54 Sir Muirhead Bone
18 Pierre Bonnard
27 Sir Frank Brangwyn
60 Ralph Brown
8 Lady Elizabeth Butler
57 Antonio Canova
8 Emily (Milly) Childers
27, 28 Sir George Clausen
13 John Constable
15 Camille Corot
13, 52 John Sell Cotman
15 Gustave Courbet
52 John Robert Cozens
13 John Crome
51 Ken Currie
40 Alan Davie
55 Tacita Dean
19 André Derain
62 Chris Drury
54 Albrecht Dürer
58 Jacob Epstein
18 Henri Fantin-Latour
29 Mark Fisher
49 Bill Fontana
41 Terry Frost
59 Naum Gabo
58 Henri Gaudier-Brzeska
23 Mark Gertler
58 Eric Gill
21 Harold Gilman
21 Charles Ginner
21 Spencer Gore
COVER Antony Gormley
39 Derrick Greaves
10 John Atkinson Grimshaw
46 Tim Head
59 Barbara Hepworth
38 Patrick Heron
29 Adriaan Josef Heymans
33 Ivon Hitchens
53 David Hockney
7 Frank Holl
7 John William Inchbold
23 Augustus John
23 Gwen John
25 Jacob Kramer
46 Susan Lacey
11 Frederic Lord Leighton
31 Percy Wyndham Lewis
14 Georges Michel
53, 59, 66 Henry Moore
34, 55 Paul Nash
35 Ben Nicholson
32 William Nicholson
1 Adelsteen Normann
7 George Bernard O'Neill
28 Sir William Orpen
60 Eduardo Paolozzi
47 Grayson Perry
55 Pablo Picasso
34 John Piper
44 Paula Rego
39 Alan Reynolds
38 Ceri Richards
54 Rembrandt van Rijn
32 William Roberts
10 Frederick Cayley Robinson
4 Auguste Rodin
61 Eva Rothschild
27 Georg Sauter
41 William Scott
28 Mark Senior
16 Walter Richard Sickert
17 Paul Signac
17 Alfred Sisley
39 Jack Smith
22 Sir Matthew Smith
29 Joaquin Sorolla y Bastida
24 Stanley Spencer
47 Georgina Starr
33 Graham Sutherland
8 James Tissot
52 Joseph Mallord William Turner
34 Edward Wadsworth
48 Mark Wallinger
14 James Ward
9 John William Waterhouse
45 Stephen Willats
61 Bill Woodrow
18 Edouard Vuillard

Copyright Acknowledgements

Every attempt has been made to contact the holders of copyright in the works illustrated and anyone believing an omission has been made should contact Leeds Art Gallery.

p1 The Sognefjord 1885
Adelsteen Normann
© Leeds Museums & Galleries

p4 The Age of Bronze 1877
Auguste Rodin
© Leeds Museums & Galleries

p7 I am the Resurrection and the Life (The Village Funeral) 1872
Frank Holl
© Leeds Museums & Galleries

Public Opinion c1863
George Bernard O'Neill
© Leeds Museums & Galleries

At Bolton (The White Doe of Rylstone) 1855
John William Inchbold
© Leeds Museums & Galleries

p8 Scotland for Ever! 1881
Lady Elizabeth Butler
© Leeds Museums & Galleries

Self Portrait 1889
Emily (Milly) Childers
© Leeds Museums & Galleries

The Bridesmaid c1885
James Tissot
© Leeds Museums & Galleries

p9 The Lady of Shalott 1894
John William Waterhouse
© Leeds Museums & Galleries

p10 Reflections on the Thames, Westminster 1880
John Atkinson Grimshaw
© Leeds Museums & Galleries

The Outward Bound 1912
Frederick Cayley Robinson
© Leeds Museums & Galleries

p11 The Return of Persephone c1891
Frederic Lord Leighton
© Leeds Museums & Galleries

p13 The Vale of Dedham 1814
John Constable
© Leeds Museums & Galleries

On the River Yare 1807
John Sell Cotman
© Leeds Museums & Galleries

Wherries on the Yare c1810
John Crome
© Leeds Museums & Galleries

p14 Storm near Montmartre
Georges Michel
© Leeds Museums & Galleries

Study for 'Gordale Scar' c1811–13
James Ward
© Leeds Museums & Galleries

p15 The Young Ladies of the Village 1851
Gustave Courbet
© Leeds Museums & Galleries

The Mont Valerian c1835
Camille Corot
© Leeds Museums & Galleries

p16 The Blackbird of Paradise c1896–98
Walter Richard Sickert
© Estate of Walter Sickert. All rights reserved, DACS 2007

p17 Autumn Evening on the River 1875
Alfred Sisley
© Leeds Museums & Galleries

The Railway Junction at Bois-Colombes (La Route Pontoise) 1886
Paul Signac
© Leeds Museums & Galleries

p18 Portrait of Mme Leon Maitre 1884
Henri Fantin-Latour
© Leeds Museums & Galleries

Mlle Grandidier in the Artist's Studio c1912
Edouard Vuillard
© Estate of Edouard Vuillard. All rights reserved, DACS 2007

Grandmother and Child 1894
Pierre Bonnard
© Estate of Pierre Bonnard. All rights reserved, DACS 2007

p19 Barges on the Thames 1906
André Derain
© Estate of André Derain. All rights reserved, DACS 2007

p21 The Circus c1913
Charles Ginner
© Leeds Museums & Galleries

The Balcony, Mornington Crescent c1911
Spencer Gore
© Leeds Museums & Galleries

Portrait of Mrs Mounter c1916–17
Harold Gilman
© Leeds Museums & Galleries

p22 Lilies c1913–14
Sir Matthew Smith
© Courtesy of the artist's estate 2007

p23 The Pond, Garsington 1916
Mark Gertler
© Courtesy of the artist's estate 2007

Portrait of Chloe Boughton-Leigh c1910–14
Gwen John
© Estate of Gwen John. All rights reserved, DACS 2007

Landscape at Chirk 1911–12
Augustus John
© Courtesy of the artist's estate 2007

p24 Christ's Entry into Jerusalem c1919
Stanley Spencer
© Estate of Sir Stanley Spencer 2007. All rights reserved, DACS 2007

p25 The Day of Atonement 1919
Jacob Kramer
© Reproduced courtesy of the Williams Roberts Society 2007

p27 The Blacksmiths 1904–05
Sir Frank Brangwyn
© Reproduced courtesy of David Brangwyn/Bridgeman Art Library 2007

A Little Child 1888
Sir George Clausen
© Reproduced courtesy of the artist's estate 2007

The Leeds Picture c1908
Georg Sauter
© Courtesy of the artist's estate 2007

p28 Reading by Lamplight 1909
Sir George Clausen
© Courtesy of the artist's estate 2007

Toil c1901
Mark Senior
© Leeds Museums & Galleries

Nude Study 1906
Sir William Orpen
© Leeds Museums & Galleries

p29 Silver Birches (Chemin de Bouleaux) c1912
Adriaan Josef Heymans
© Leeds Museums & Galleries

Ladies on the Beach 1906
Joaquin Sorolla y Bastida
© Leeds Museums & Galleries

The Waterways c1906
Mark Fisher
© Leeds Museums & Galleries

p31 Praxitella c1921
Percy Wyndham Lewis
© Reproduced courtesy of the artist's estate 2007

p32 The Dance Club 1923
William Roberts
© Reproduced courtesy of the Williams Roberts Society 2007

On the Downs 1924
William Nicholson
© Reproduced courtesy of the William Nicholson Trust 2007

p33 Sunrise Between the Hedges 1939
Graham Sutherland
© Reproduced courtesy of the artist's estate 2007

Hazel Wood 1944
Ivon Hitchens
© Reproduced courtesy of the artist's estate 2007

p34 Circle of the Monoliths c1938
Paul Nash
© Reproduced courtesy of Tate Britain 2007

Requiescat 1940
Edward Wadsworth
© Estate of Edward Wadsworth. All rights reserved, DACS 2007

Dead Resort, Kempton c1939
John Piper
© Reproduced courtesy of the artist's estate 2007

p35 Painting 1940
Ben Nicholson
© Estate of Ben Nicholson. All rights reserved, DACS 2007

p37 Painting 1950
Francis Bacon
© Estate of Francis Bacon/ARS, NY and DACS, London 2007

p38 Anemones and Lemons 1950
Patrick Heron
© Estate of Patrick Heron. All rights reserved, DACS 2007

The Deposition of Christ 1958
Ceri Richards
© Estate of Ceri Richards. All rights reserved, DACS 2007

p39 Children on Steps c1956
Derrick Greaves
© Reproduced courtesy of the artist 2007

Outbuildings Pastorale 1952
Alan Reynolds
© Reproduced courtesy of the artist/Annely Juda Fine Art Gallery 2007

Still Life with Bowl of Cherries 1954–55
Jack Smith
© Reproduced courtesy of the artist/Angela Flowers, Flowers East Gallery 2007

p40 In the Face of the Witch 1955
Alan Davie
© Reproduced courtesy of the artist 2007

Maples Demolition, Euston Road 1960
Frank Auerbach
© Reproduced courtesy of the artist/Marlborough Fine Art 2007

p41 Brown Verticals c1958–59
Terry Frost
© Reproduced courtesy of the artist's estate/ Bridgeman Art Library 2007

Blue Still Life c1957
William Scott
© Reproduced courtesy of the artist's estate 2007

p43 Helios 1990
Gillian Ayres
© Reproduced courtesy of the artist 2007

p44 The Artist in Her Studio 1993
Paula Rego
© Reproduced courtesy of the artist/Marlborough Fine Art 2007

p45 Doppelgänger 1984
Stephen Willats
© Reproduced courtesy of the artist 2007

p46 Whisper the Wind the Waves 1993
Susan Lacy
© Reproduced courtesy of the artist 2007

Erasers 1985
Tim Head
© Reproduced courtesy of the artist 2007

p47 Big V 2004
Georgina Starr
© Reproduced courtesy of the artist 2007

What Things Say About Us 2002
Grayson Perry
© Reproduced courtesy of the artist/Victoria Miro Gallery 2007

p48 Threshold to the Kingdom 2000
Mark Wallinger
© Reproduced courtesy of the artist 2007

p49 Primal Soundings 2004
Bill Fontana
© Reproduced courtesy of the artist 2007

p51 In the City Bar... Disillusion 1985
Ken Currie
© Reproduced courtesy of the artist/Angela Flowers, Flowers East Gallery 2007

p52 Lake Albano and Castel Gandolfo
John Robert Cozens
© Leeds Museums & Galleries

The Valley of the Washburn c1818
Joseph Mallord William Turner
© Leeds Museums & Galleries

Barnard Castle from Towler Hill c1806
John Sell Cotman
© Leeds Museums & Galleries

p53 Shelter Scene – Two Seated Figures 1941
Henry Moore
© Reproduced by kind permission of the Henry Moore Foundation 2007

Peter Reading in Anguillara 1967
David Hockney
© Reproduced courtesy of the artist/Annely Juda Fine Art Gallery 2007

p54 Nemesis (The Great Fortune) c1501–02
Albrecht Dürer
© Leeds Museums & Galleries

York Road, Leeds
Sir Muirhead Bone
© Reproduced courtesy of the artist 2007

The Negress Lying Down 1658
Rembrandt van Rijn
© Leeds Museums & Galleries

p55 Le Repas Frugal (The Frugal Meal) 1913
Pablo Picasso
© Estate of Pablo Picasso. All rights reserved, DACS 2007

The Book of Genesis 1924
Paul Nash
© Reproduced courtesy of Tate Britain 2007

Blind Pan 2004
Tacita Dean
© Reproduced courtesy of the artist 2007

p57 Venus 1817–20
Antonio Canova
© Leeds Museums & Galleries

p58 Maternity 1910
Jacob Epstein
© Reproduced courtesy of the artist's estate 2007

Mother and Child 1910
Eric Gill
© Reproduced by kind permission Eric Gill Society 2007

The Wrestler 1912
Henri Gaudier-Brzeska
© Leeds Museums & Galleries

p59 Reclining Figure 1929
Henry Moore
© Reproduced by kind permission of the Henry Moore Foundation 2007

Configuration (Phira) 1955
Barbara Hepworth
© Reproduced courtesy of the artist's estate 2007

Construction in Space: Soaring 1930
Naum Gabo
© Reproduced courtesy of the artist/Annely Juda Fine Art Gallery 2007

p60 Running Girl with Wheel 1954
Ralph Brown
© Reproduced courtesy of the artist 2007

Poem for the Trio MRT 1964
Eduardo Paolozzi
© Estate of Eduardo Paolozzi. All rights reserved, DACS 2007

p61 Twin-Tub with Beaver 1981
Bill Woodrow
© Reproduced courtesy of the artist 2007

Fruit of Oblivion 1982
Edward Allington
© Reproduced courtesy of the artist 2007

Bad Hat 2002
Eva Rothschild
© Reproduced courtesy of the artist 2007

p62 Medicine Wheel 1982–83
Chris Drury
© Reproduced courtesy of the artist/Victoria Miro Gallery 2007

p66 Reclining Woman '80 No.1
Henry Moore
© Reproduced by kind permission of the Henry Moore Foundation 2007